How to Create Math Experts with
Pattern Blocks

Peggy McLean and Lyle Lee Jenkins

Perfect School Collection™

To contact the authors regarding keynotes, workshops or bulk material orders visit www.LtoJ.net/Contact

ISBN: 978-1-956457-10-0

Book Design & Graphics: Christy Courtright, Christy's Customs LLC
Quality Assurance Manager: Kelly Lippert
Publishing Consultant: Martha Bullen, Bullen Publishing Services
Distribution Coordinator: Maggie McLaughlin

Printed in the United States of America

The Perfect School Collection™

How to Create a Perfect School by Lyle Lee Jenkins

How to Create a Perfect Home School by Lyle Lee Jenkins and Kelly Hawkinson Lippert

Perfect School Collection™ Resources

How to Create Math Experts series by Peggy McLean and Lyle Lee Jenkins

How to Create Math Experts with Fluency Quizzes by Peggy McLean and Lyle Lee Jenkins

How to Create Math Experts with Math Standards Quizzes by Peggy McLean, Laura Hayes and Lyle Lee Jenkins

How to Create a Math Foundation for Future Math Experts by Lyle Lee Jenkins

How to Create Language Experts with Literary Terms series by Codi Hrouda and Emma McInerney with Lyle Lee Jenkins

How to Create Bible Experts: Genesis to Revelation by Richard Douglas Junior Jenkins with Lyle Lee Jenkins

Young Readers

Bible Patterns for Young Readers series by Lyle Lee Jenkins

Aesop Patterns for Young Readers series by Lyle Lee Jenkins

Young Authors

Wordless Books for Young Authors series by Jim Chansler and Lyle Lee Jenkins

Special Project

All About Henry: Rich Widower of Savannah Valley by Lyle Lee Jenkins

CONTENTS

Introduction

PEGGY MCLEAN AND LYLE LEE JENKINS created a series of elementary math books to offer teachers proven resources for helping children master essential math concepts. Each book guides children to gain powerful lifelong math insights. Confidence builds more and more as children increase their math skills and knowledge from a young age. *How to Create Math Experts with Pattern Blocks* is true to its title. Adults and children are amazed at what they learn from this powerful, colorful set of six shapes.

The books subtitle, *Constant Thrill from Success*, does not mean immediate thrill or immediate success. When people are intrinsically motivated they work hard, and the thrill comes from the learning. The authors' aim is for students to be 100% engaged and love learning. The biggest thrill usually comes from a struggle over several days to finally solve a problem.

How to Create Math Experts with Pattern Blocks is included within **The Perfect School Collection™** because it is an immense help in preserving intrinsic motivation. Lyle Lee Jenkins defines a perfect school as one in which the intrinsic motivation children bring with them to kindergarten is maintained for the next 12 years.

The metaphor of a tree with roots illustrates the process of children developing new skills. Images of trees rarely include the roots because they are hidden from view. However, we all know that if the roots die, it won't be long until the visible tree dies. John Hattie's "skill, will and thrill" learning model captures the thoughts behind the tree with roots. The visible tree is the math skill to be learned with Pattern Blocks. The invisible roots represent the will and the thrill maintaining students' natural love of learning. When students' natural love of learning (intrinsic motivation) is destroyed, it is not very long before the visible tree (skills) falters and dies. That is why math skills must be learned in such an exciting way that children's intrinsic motivation is maintained at a very high level!

Adults and high school students were asked to estimate how many high school students are as excited about school learning as they once were as kindergartners. The research shows that 5 to 8% of students keep this love of learning for 13 years of K - 12 education. We can do better. The Perfect School Collection™ books will greatly increase this percentage.

Children can play with hammers, screw drivers, and levels, but adults do not call those objects toys. Children can also play with Pattern Blocks, but it would be a mistake to call them toys; they are tools just like rulers, compasses, and protractors. In fact, Pattern Blocks are one of the most powerful tools ever invented to give children a solid understanding of geometry, logic, measurement, equations, and fractions.

The thrill of learning does not come from remembering rules and formulas often taught in math and phonics. It comes from children figuring out solutions on their own. Pattern Blocks and accompanying mirrors are the tools for thrilling learning. When children record their answers with the Pattern Block template, it is comparable to family photographs from an event. Reproducing Pattern Block answers with the template is remarkably like a family photograph: memories are preserved.

As mentioned earlier, the problems in *How to Create Math Experts with Pattern Blocks* might not be solved instantly. When children are stumped and have no more energy for the task at hand, we suggest they move on to something else. We all know that solutions to adult problems often occur when not thinking directly about the problem. The solution can "pop into our heads" while in the shower, driving the car, or while we are on a walk or run. The same is true for children. While riding a bike, lying in bed or sitting in the back seat of the car, children can have an "aha moment" and can hardly wait to get a hold of the Pattern Blocks and see if their "aha" is correct. When it is, we call this thrilling success.

Thrill does not come from an adult placing a check mark by a problem that is incorrect. When an adult is looking over a student's work, the adult should place a "c" by correct answers and a simple dot by incorrect ones. The dot means temporarily wrong. When the children correct the mistake, the "c" covers up the dot, and all problems on the page have the "c". A paper with all c's can be proudly shared with parents and other important people in the child's life.

Constant thrill from success will become your and your students' reality with *How to Create Math Experts with Pattern Blocks*.

Materials Needed:

Set of 250 Pattern Blocks (wooden or plastic)
Pattern Block Template
Clear Spinner
Plastic Mirror
Hinged Double Mirror

Available from Amazon or EAIeducation.com

Create other letters for initials, names, animals, and other interests.

You can make more
numerals.

TRAPEZOID COVER-UP GAME SPINNERS

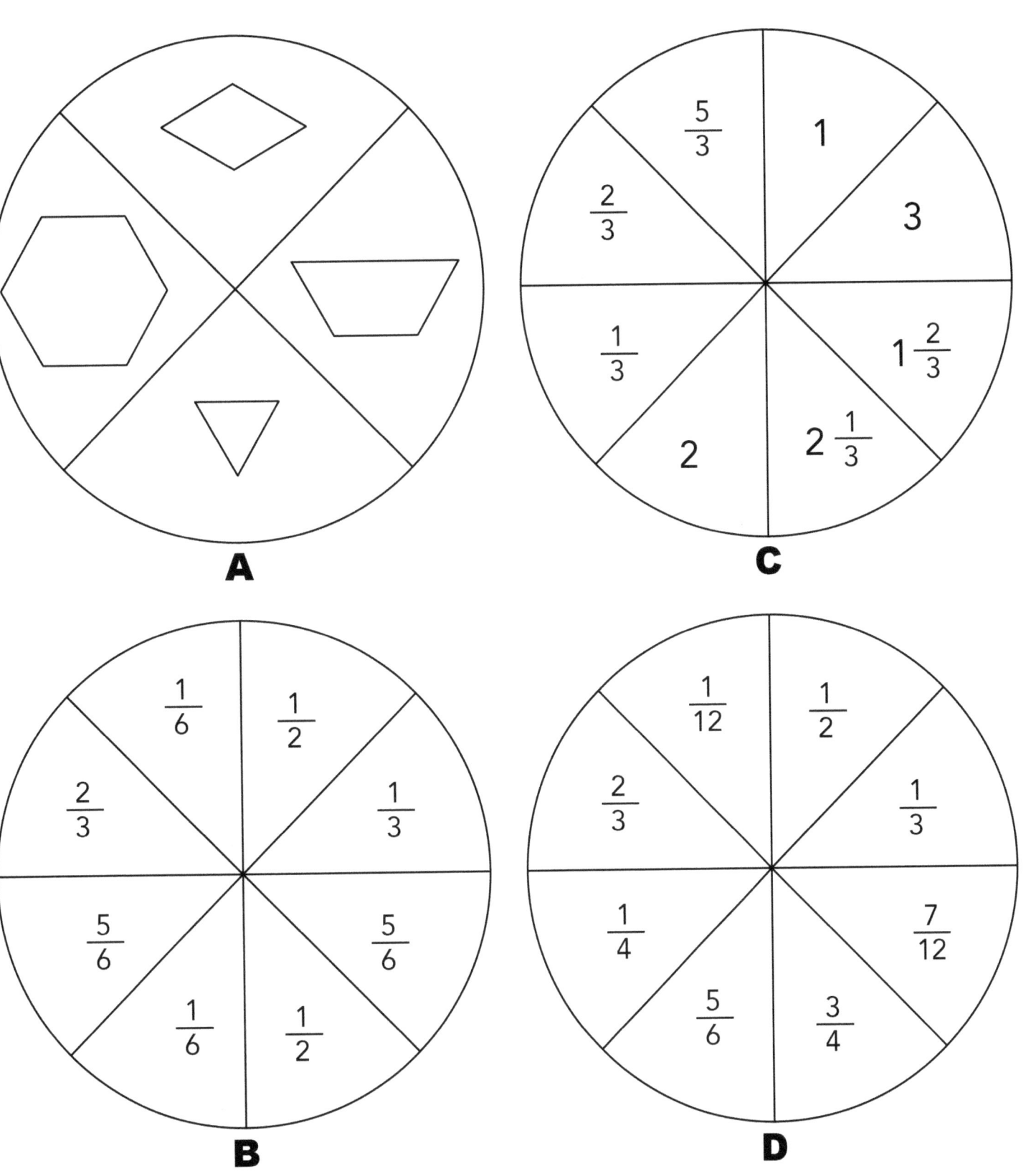

A

C

B

D

Directions

Each player receives one Trapezoid Cover Up Game Board. Players take turns spinning the spinner to determine which Pattern Block is selected.

Blocks are placed on the board. The first student to finish covering the board is the winner. For this game the four pieces are the triangle, trapezoid, wide rhombus, and hexagon.

The four spinners become increasingly more difficult from A to D, but they use the same board and Pattern Blocks. Beginners should start with A. As the students improve, they can move up to the other spinners.

- **Spinner A** is for the youngest children to spin and pick up the correct Pattern Block.
- **Spinner B** uses fractions. The hexagon is worth 1 with the 3 other pieces being a fraction of the hexagon.
- **Spinner C** has the hexagon as worth 1 with the other three pieces being less than 1.
- **Spinner D** has two hexagons as worth 1. The remaining 3 pieces are all a fraction of the size of two hexagons together.

TRAPEZOID COVER-UP
GAME BOARD

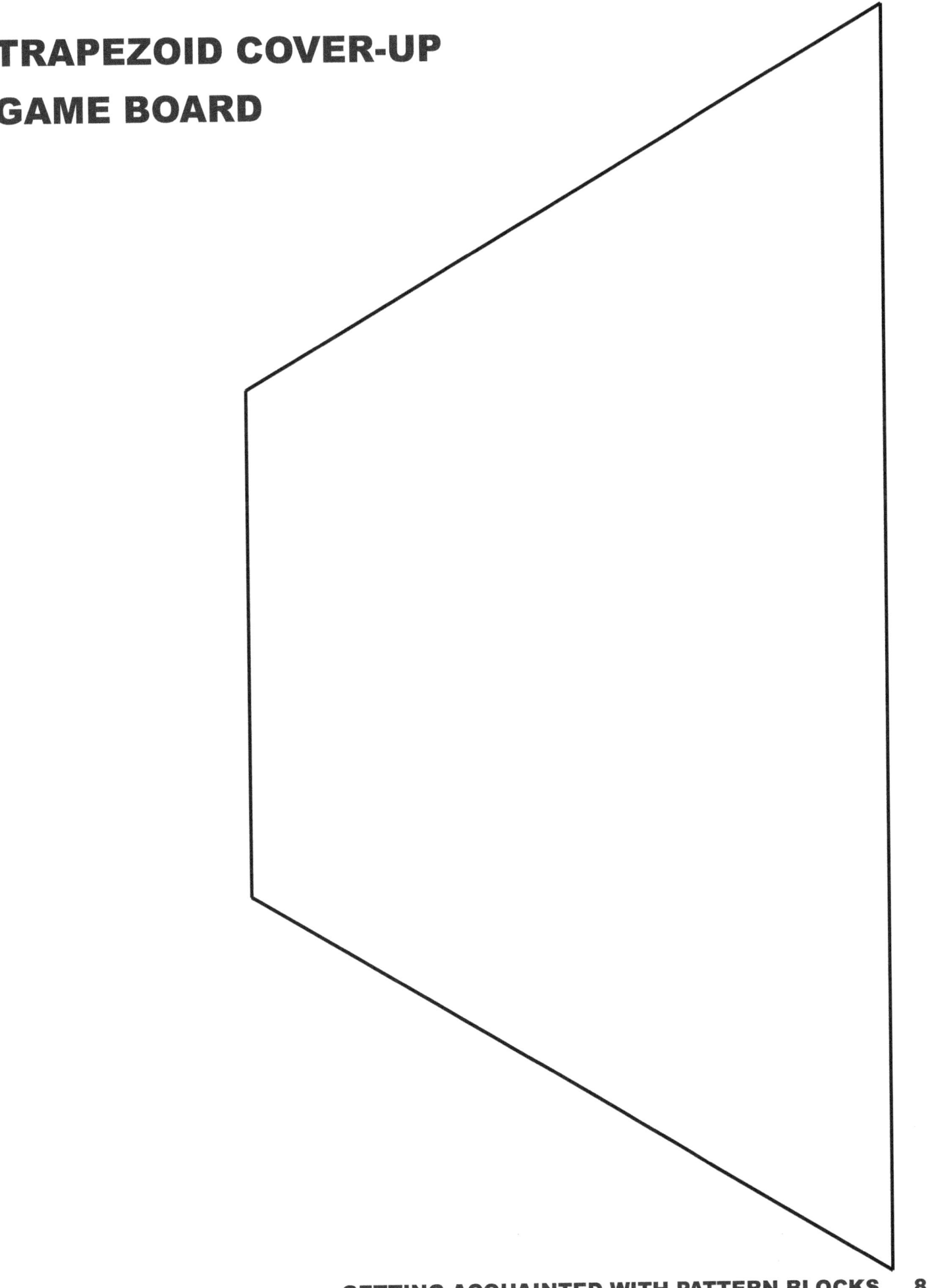

GETTING ACQUAINTED WITH PATTERN BLOCKS:
LET'S TRY SOME SHAPE PUZZLES

Cover each shape with 4 Pattern Blocks

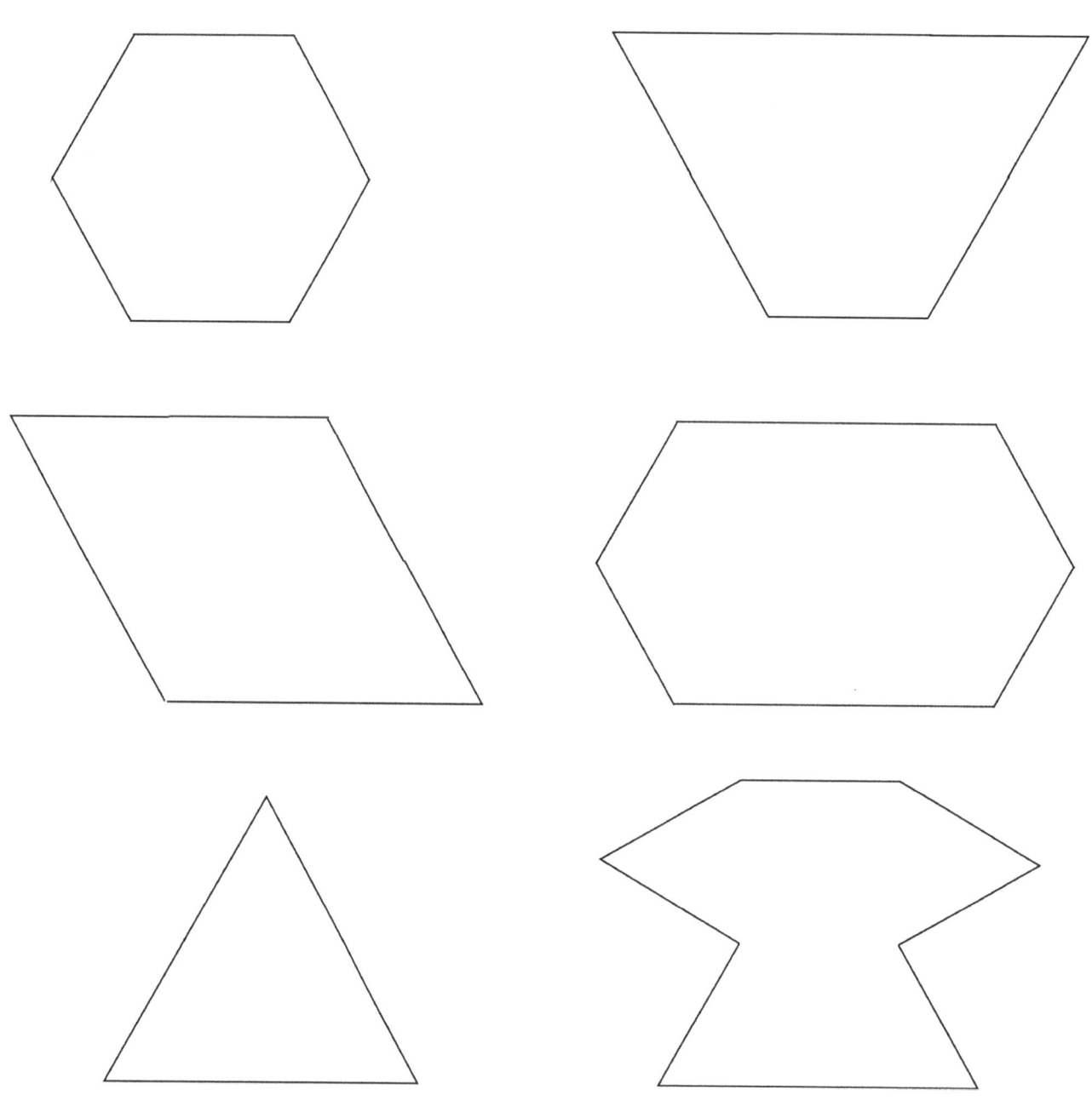

GETTING ACQUAINTED WITH
PATTERN BLOCKS:
LET'S TRY SOME MORE SHAPE PUZZLES

Cover each shape with 5 Pattern Blocks

GETTING ACQUAINTED WITH PATTERN BLOCKS:
LET'S TRY EVEN MORE SHAPE PUZZLES

Cover each shape with 6 Pattern Blocks

GETTING ACQUAINTED WITH PATTERN BLOCKS:
LET'S TRY HEXAGON PUZZLES

2 Blocks 1 Color

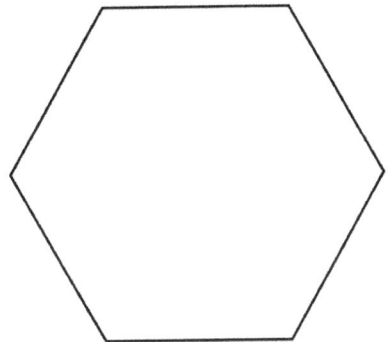

3 Blocks 3 Colors

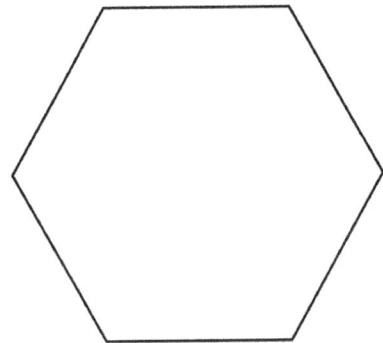

3 Blocks 1 Color

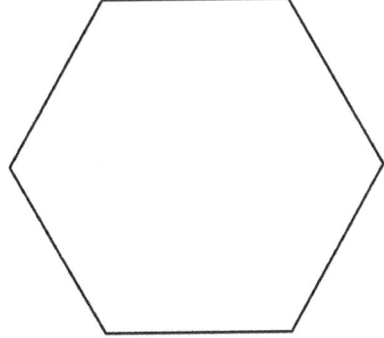

5 Blocks 2 Colors

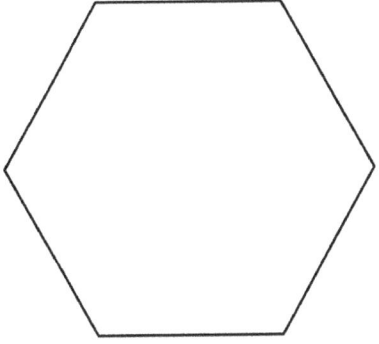

6 Blocks 1 Color

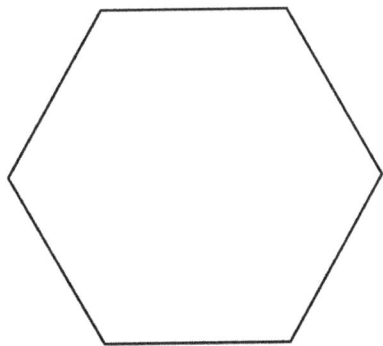

4 Blocks 2 Colors

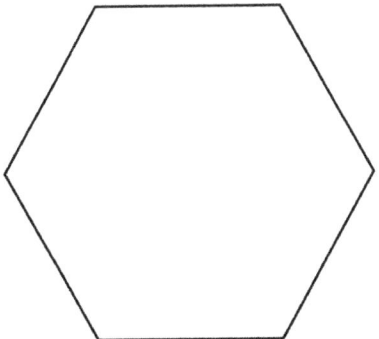

GETTING ACQUAINTED WITH PATTERN BLOCKS:
LET'S TRY TRIANGLE PUZZLES

4 Blocks 2 Colors

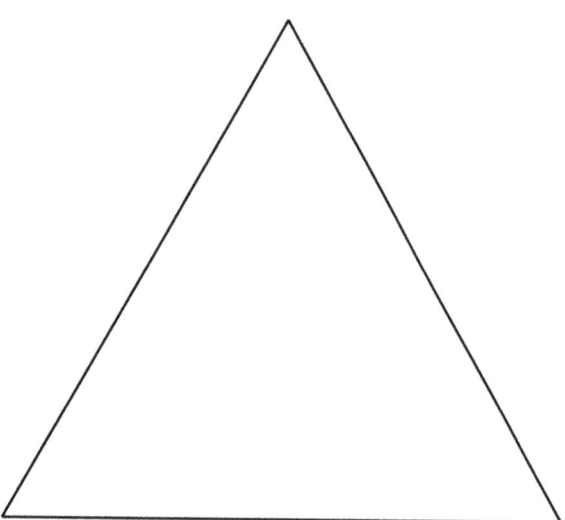

3 Blocks 1 Color

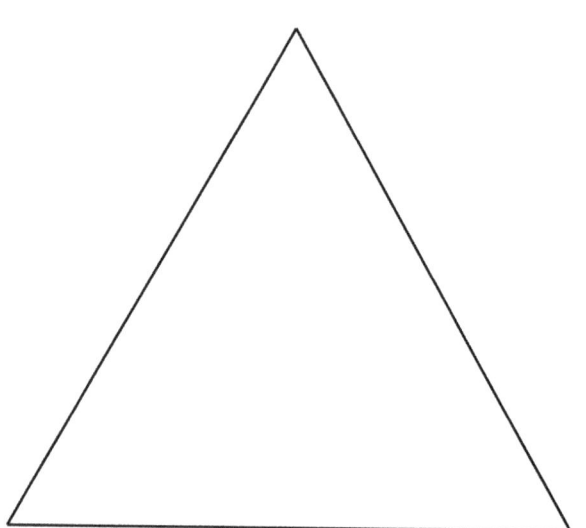

5 Blocks 3 Colors

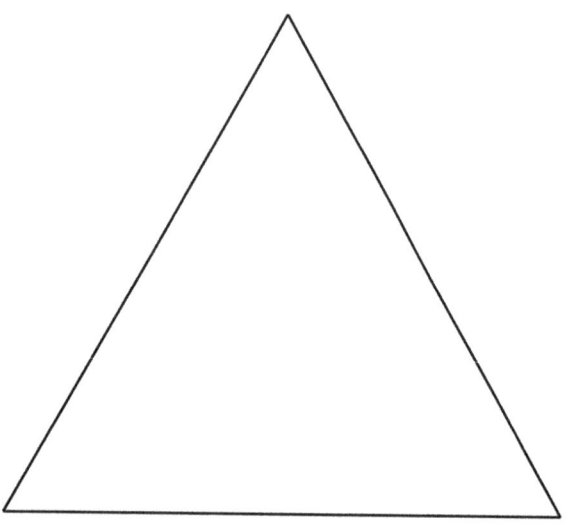

6 Blocks 2 Colors

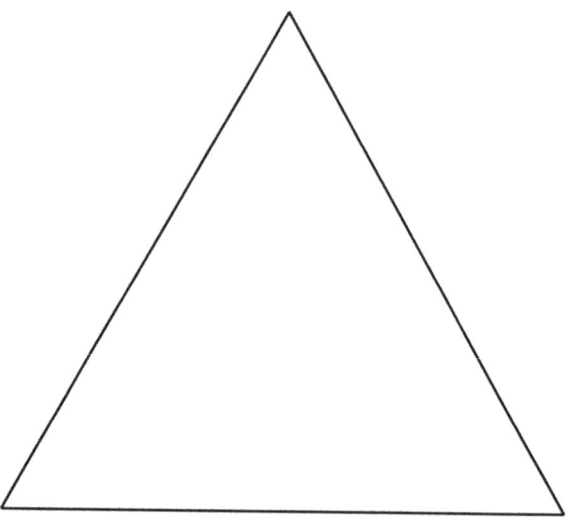

GETTING ACQUAINTED WITH PATTERN BLOCKS:
LET'S TRY TRAPEZOID PUZZLES

4 Blocks 1 Color

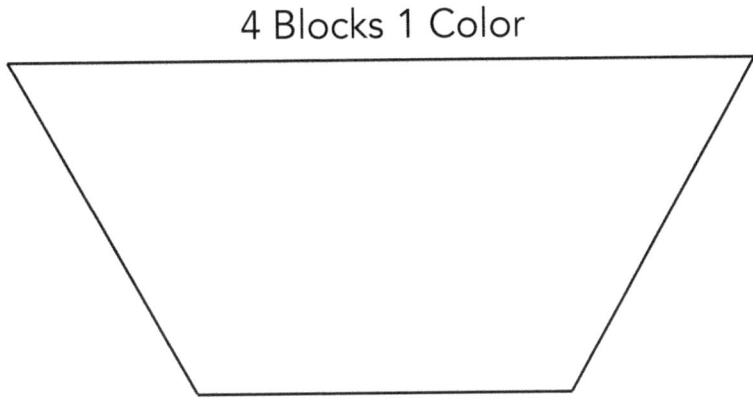

5 Blocks 3 Colors

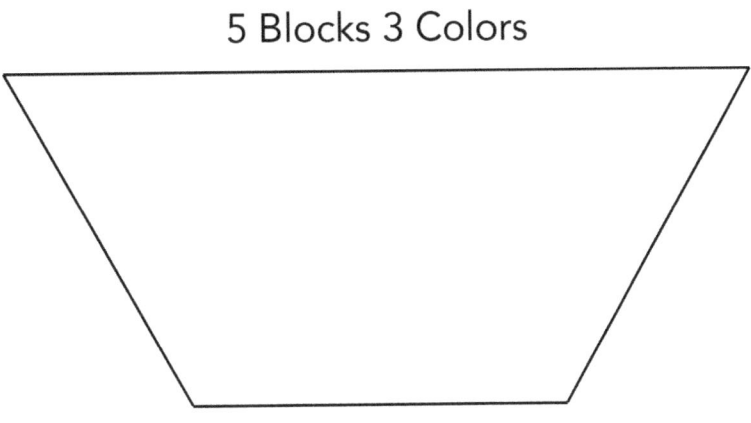

6 Blocks 3 Colors

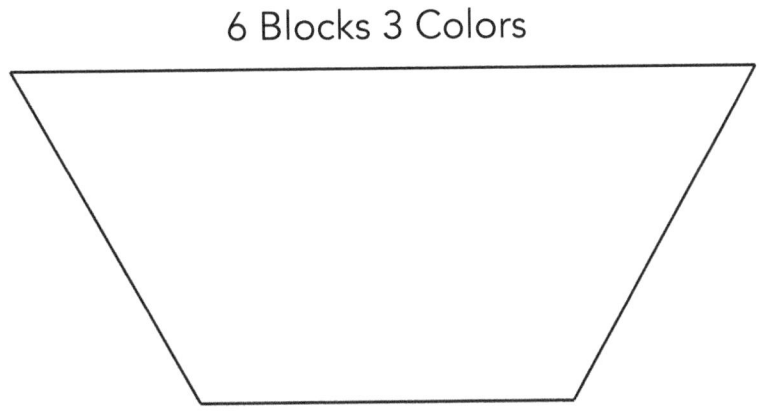

GETTING ACQUAINTED WITH PATTERN BLOCKS:
LET'S TRY RHOMBUS PUZZLES

4 Blocks 1 Color

4 Blocks 3 Colors

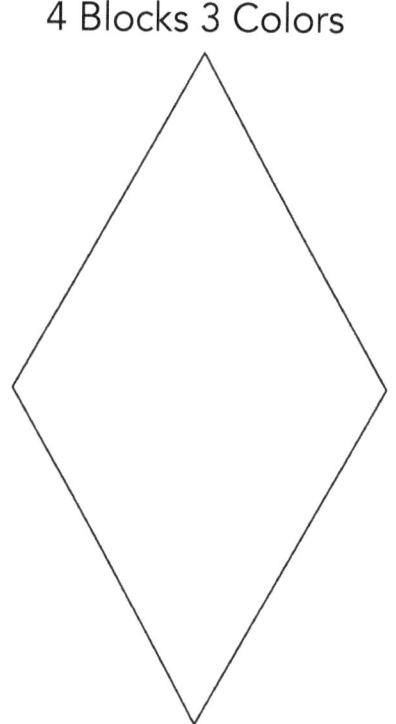

3 Blocks 2 Colors

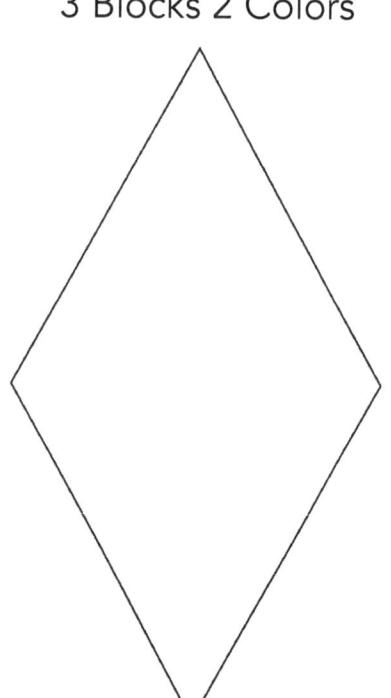

6 Blocks 2 Colors

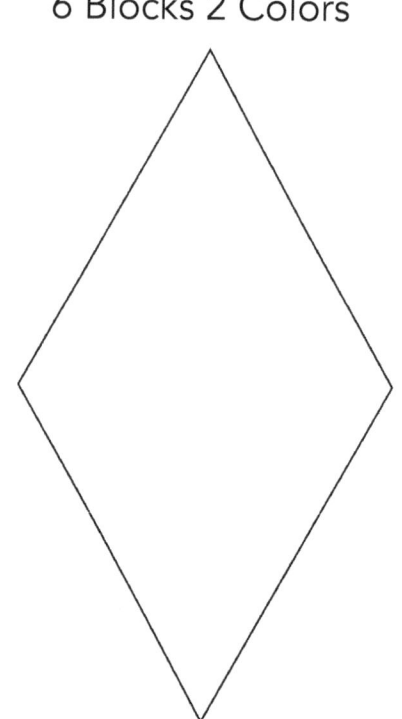

GETTING ACQUAINTED WITH PATTERN BLOCKS:
LET'S TRY OCTAGON PUZZLES

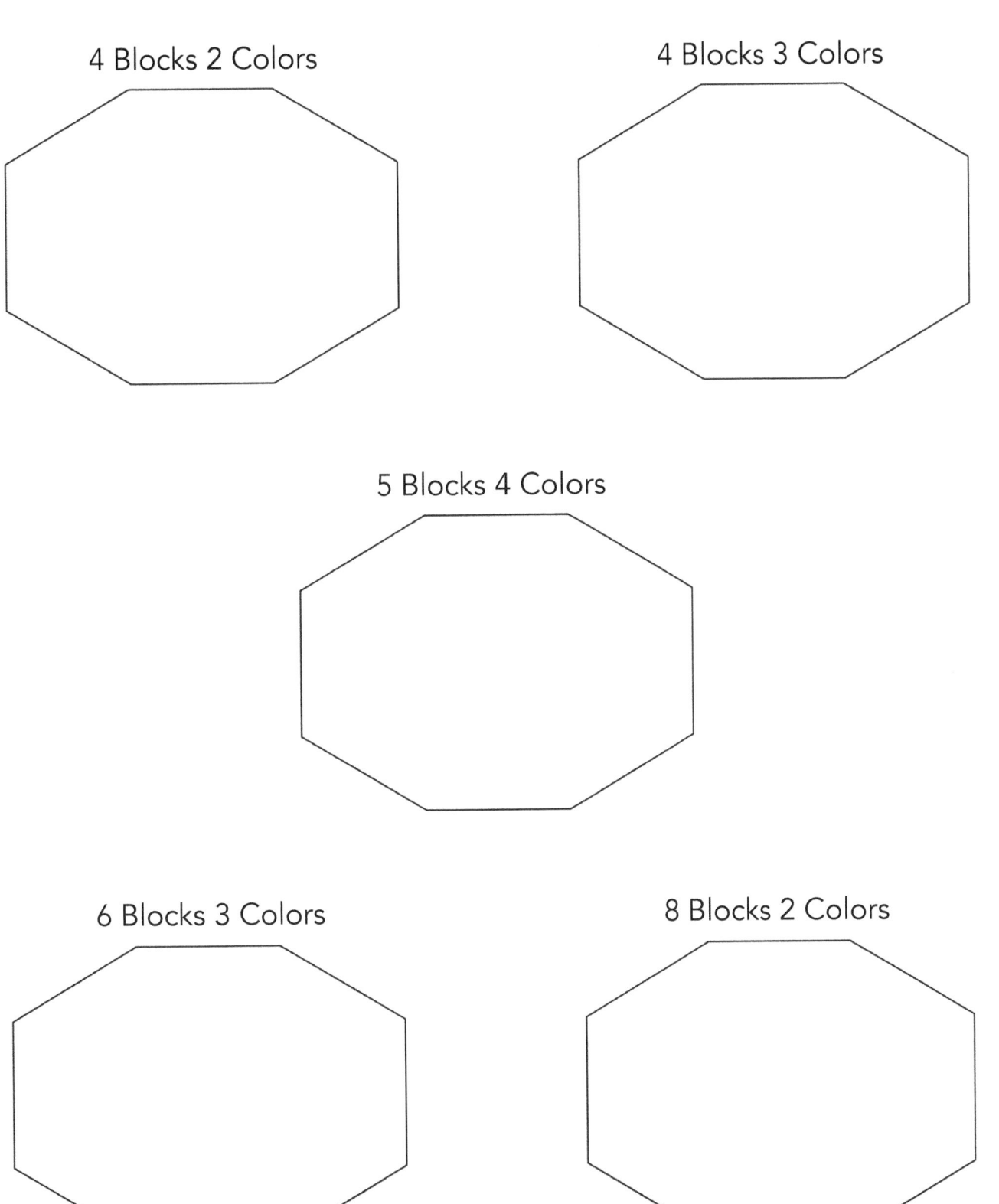

4 Blocks 2 Colors

4 Blocks 3 Colors

5 Blocks 4 Colors

6 Blocks 3 Colors

8 Blocks 2 Colors

GETTING ACQUAINTED WITH
PATTERN BLOCKS:
LET'S TRY MORE HEXAGON PUZZLES

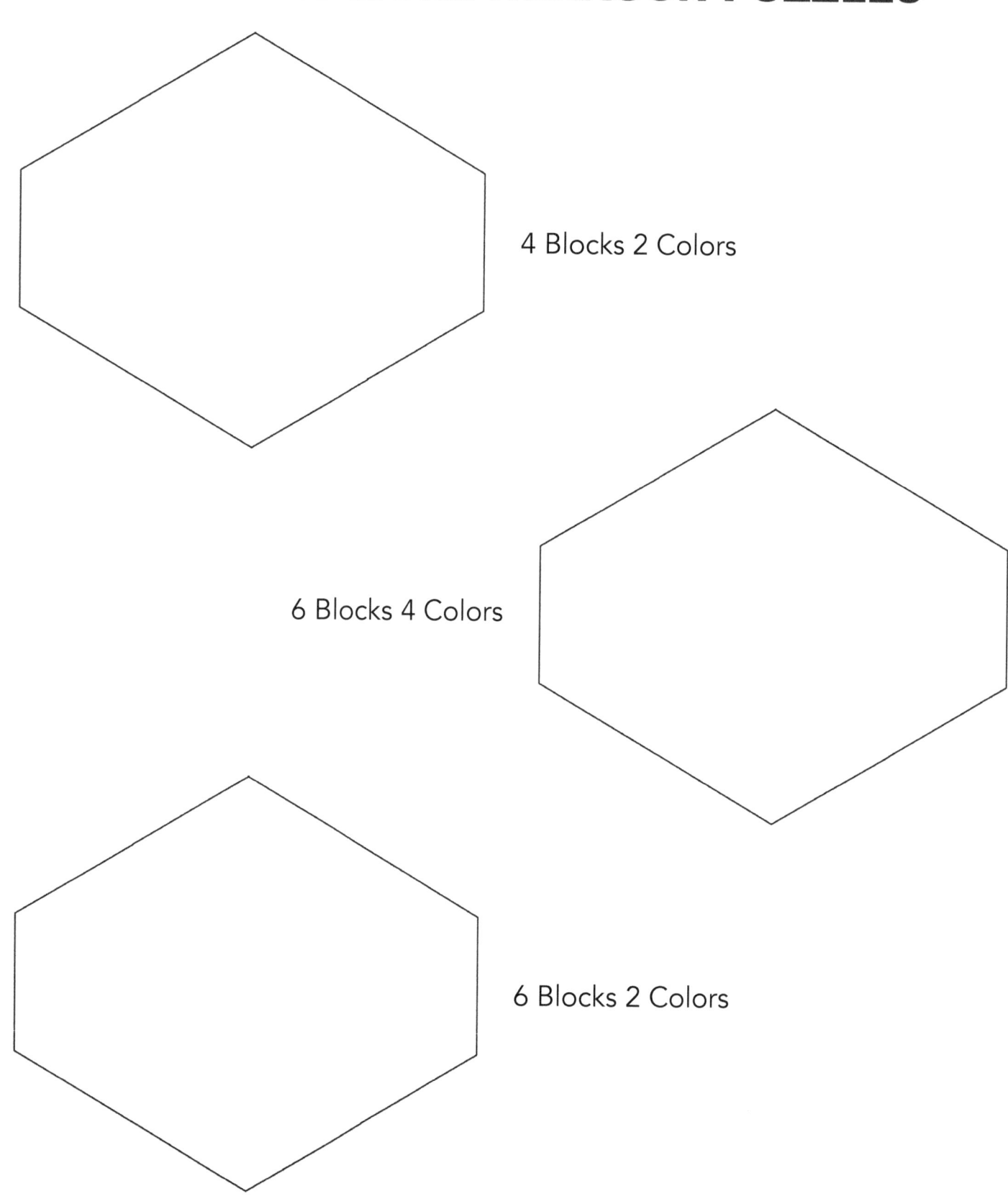

4 Blocks 2 Colors

6 Blocks 4 Colors

6 Blocks 2 Colors

BUILD AN ANIMAL; FOLLOW THE LEADER

Two students sit at a table facing each other. Each has a blank sheet of paper in front of them and a barrier is placed between them so they cannot see each other's paper. One student is the "leader" who places a Pattern Block on the paper and describes which block is on the paper and the location of the block. The second student, who cannot look at the leader's paper, listens and places a block on his/her paper.

The second student then becomes the "leader" and adds another block on his/her paper and describes the block and location. This second block may be in a completely new location, adjacent to the first block or on top of the first block.

The process continues with students taking turns being the "leader" and adding blocks. After each student has added 6 or more blocks, the barrier is removed and students compare. It will be fun to name the two designs. They could be twins if both are the same, cousins if they are close, or friends if they are completely different.

As students become more familiar with the process, they can even place blocks on the page by standing them on an edge.

Encourage students to use vocabulary of hexagon, rhombus, triangle, square, trapezoid, wide rhombus and thin rhombus as they describe their addition to the design/animal.

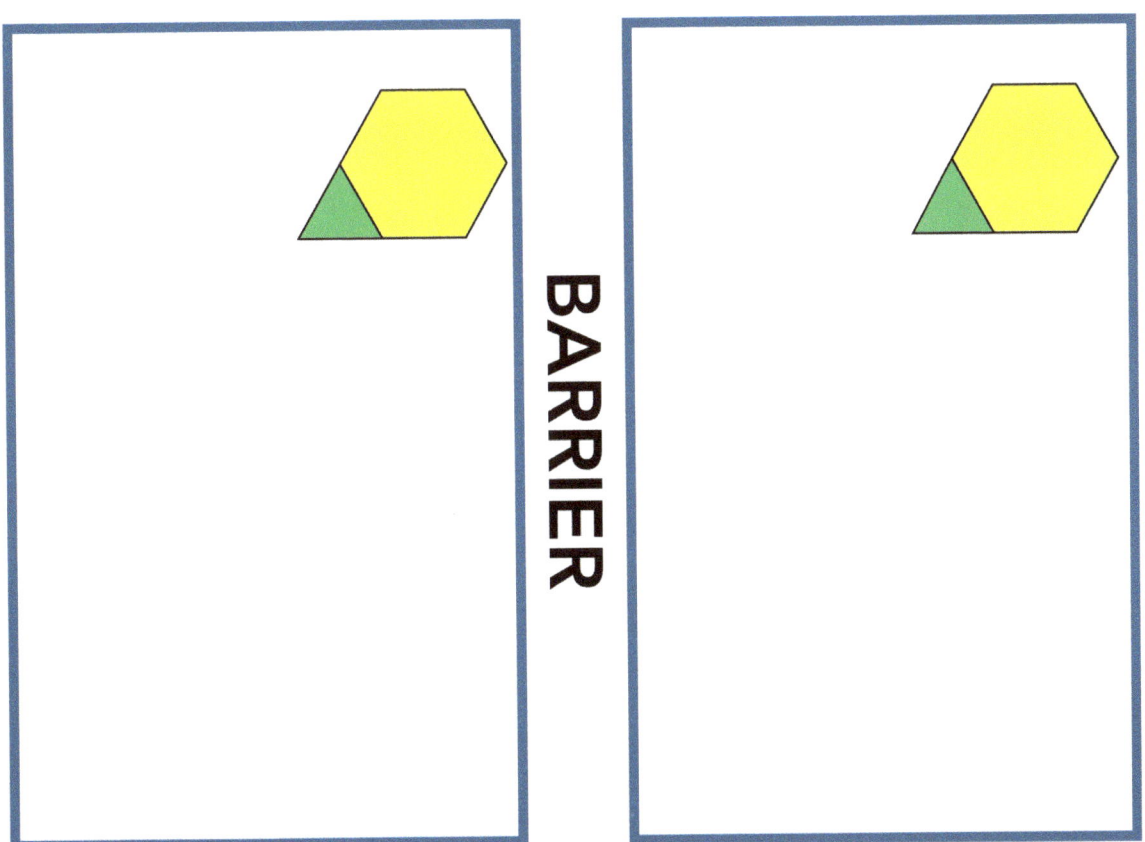

EQUATIONS WITH PATTERN BLOCKS

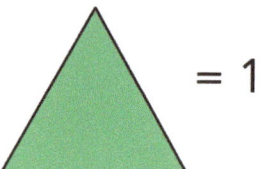 = 1

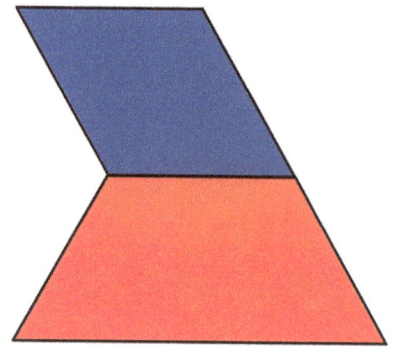

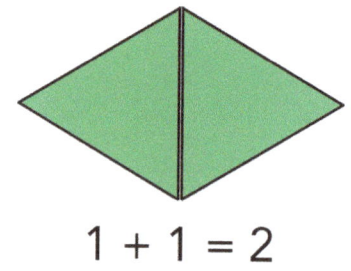

1 + 1 = 2

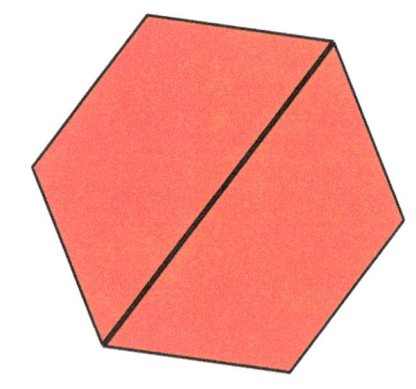

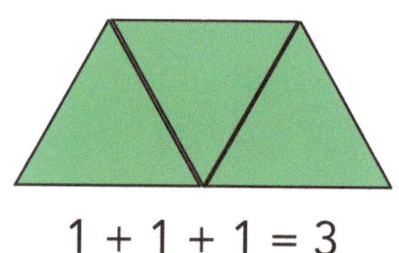

1 + 1 + 1 = 3

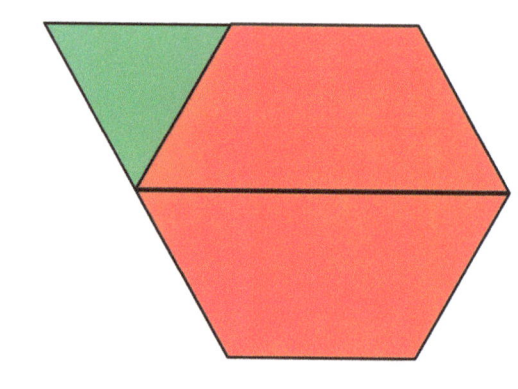

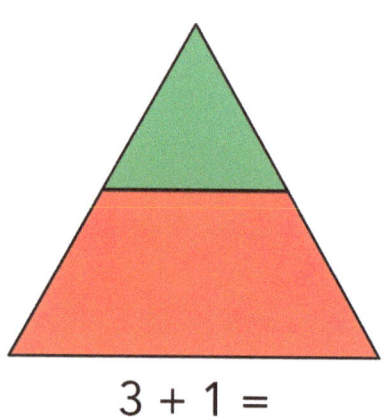

3 + 1 =

MORE EQUATIONS WITH PATTERN BLOCKS

How many ways can you make 10? 15?

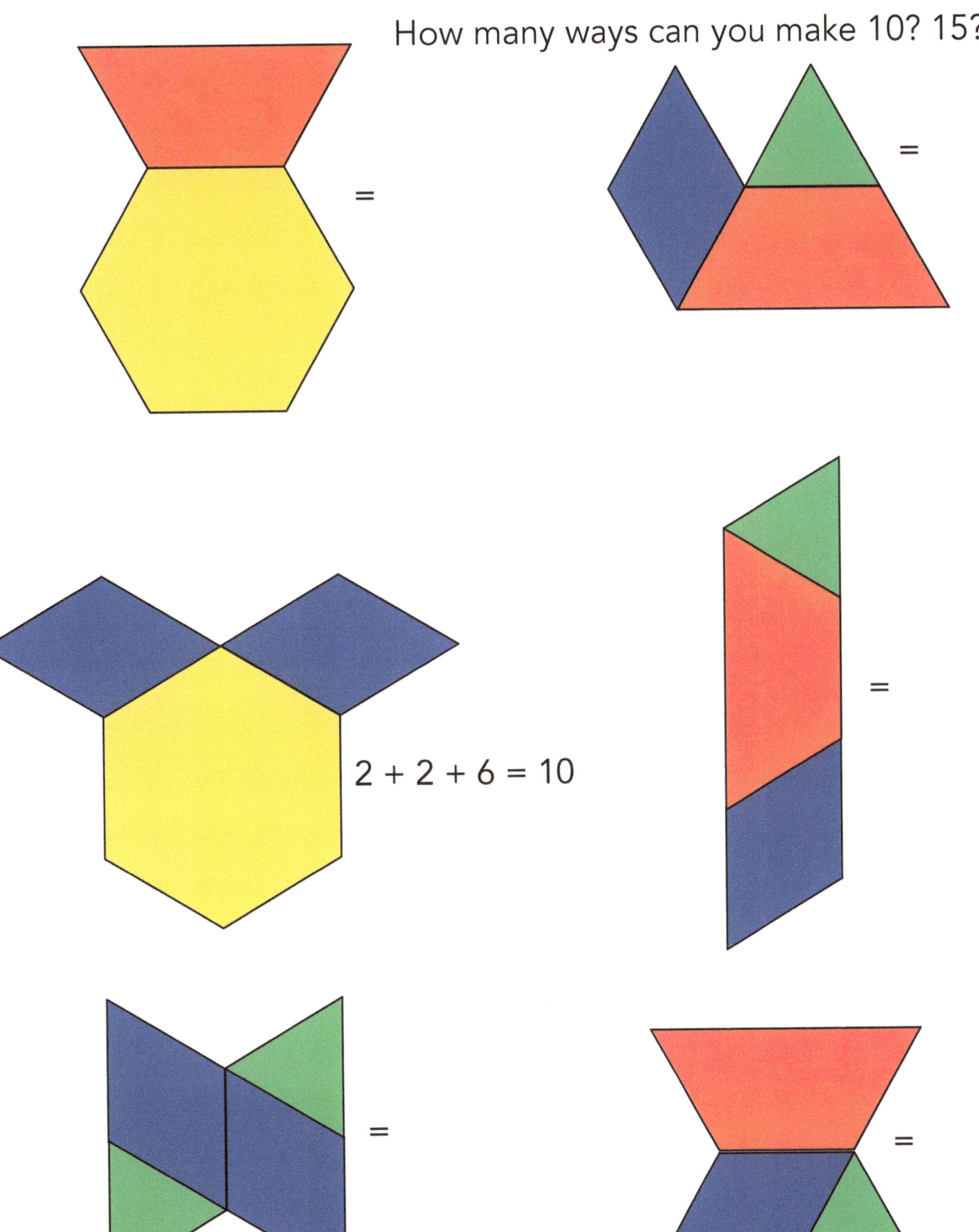

2 + 2 + 6 = 10

STRATEGY WITH THE CAT

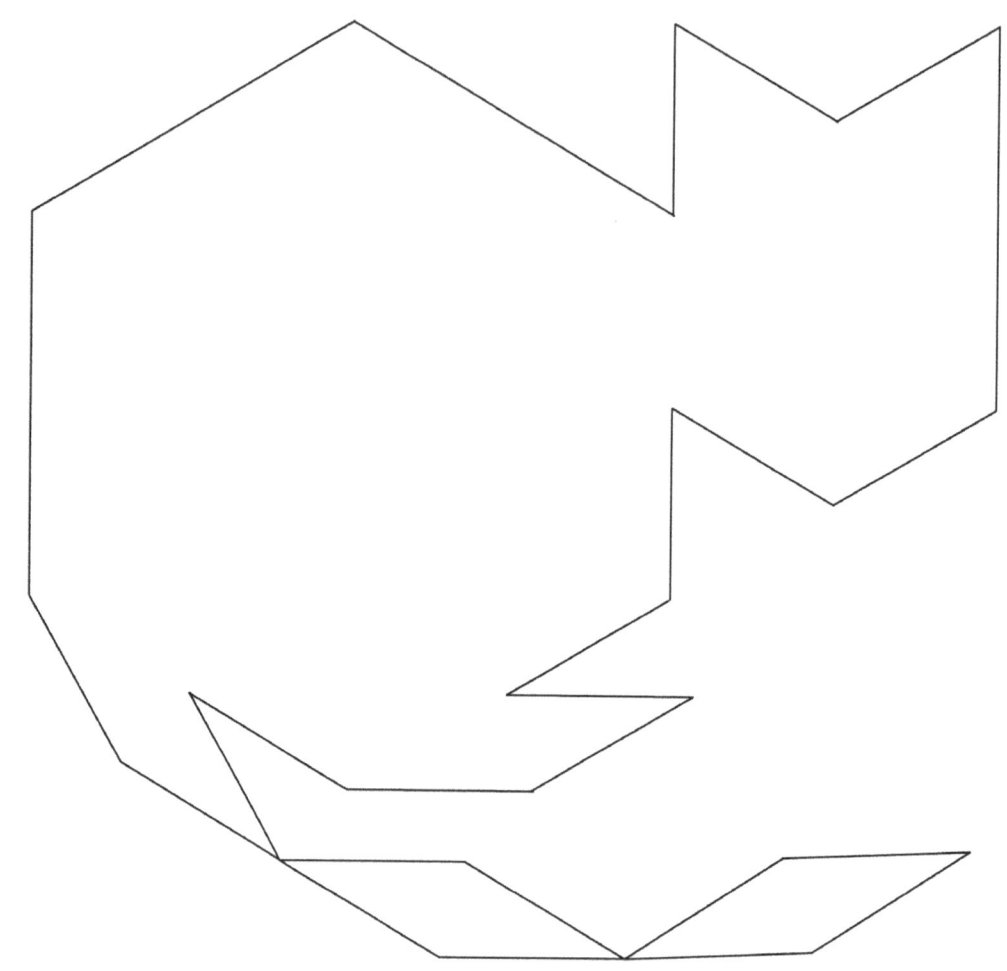

How many blocks cover the cat? Circle all possible correct answers.

1   2   3   4   5   6   7   8   9   10

11   12   13   14   15   16   17   18   19   20

21   22   23   24   25   26   27   28   29   30

31   32   33   34   35   36   37   38   39   40

STRATEGY: WHAT NUMBERS?

A. Pick up these pieces:
   What numbers can you make using only these pieces?

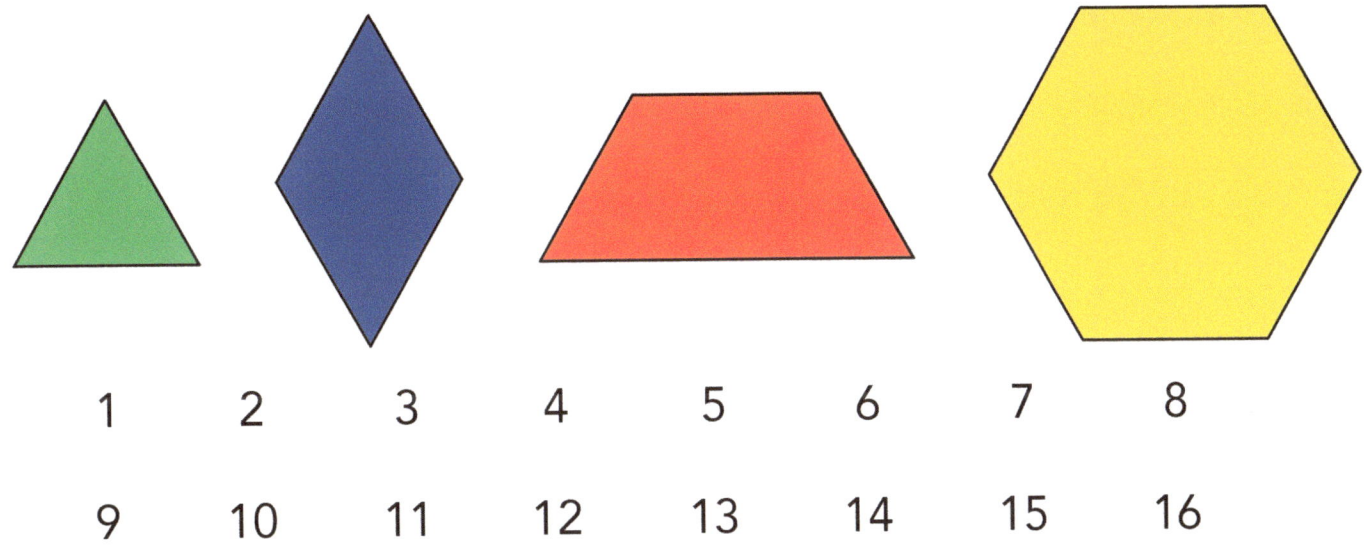

1	2	3	4	5	6	7	8
9	10	11	12	13	14	15	16

B. Pick up these pieces:
   What numbers can you make using only these pieces?

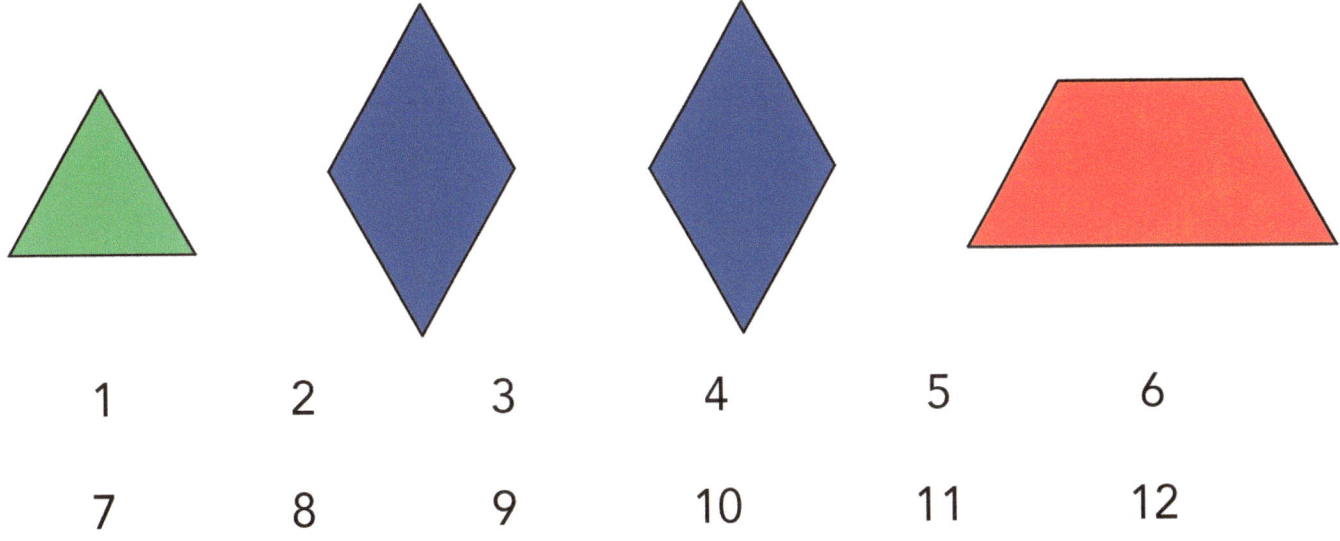

1	2	3	4	5	6
7	8	9	10	11	12

STRATEGY GAME: BLOCK - IT

Each player receives twelve blocks.
Three of each of the following colors: Green, Blue, Red, and Yellow.

Point Value for Each Color
Green = 1   Blue = 2   Red = 3   Yellow = 6

The game begins with one yellow hexagon placed on the playing surface.

The first player places any of their blocks so that one side of the block is completely touching one side of the yellow hexagon. The scoring for each play is the sum of the values for the block played and the blocks that are touching the block played.

1st Play
Player "A" selected a green triangle to play. Therefore yellow and green blocks are touching so the points are scored: 6 + 1 = 7

Scoring Sheet, Player A
1) 7
2) ____ ____

2nd Play
Player "B" selected a red trapezoid to play. Because it is touching one full side of the yellow hexagon and one full side of the green triangle, the score is 10 points: 6 + 1 + 3 = 10

Scoring Sheet, Player B
1) 10
2) ____ ____

3rd Play
Player "A" selected a blue rhombus to play. Scoring is 8 points since blue and yellow sides are touching: 6 + 2 = 8

Scoring Sheet, Player A
1) 7
2) 8   15
3) ____ ____

4th Play
Player "B" selected a green triangle to play. Scoring is 6 points since 2 blocks are touching one complete side of the triangle: 1 + 2 + 3 = 6

Scoring Sheet, Player A
1) 10
2) 6   16
3) ____ ____

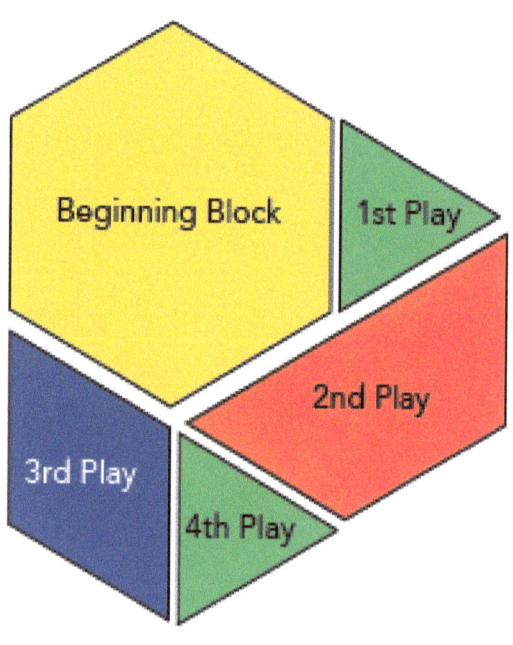

You continue to play until all the players have used all of their blocks.

BLOCK - IT SCORING SHEET

1) _____

2) _____   _____

3) _____   _____

4) _____   _____

5) _____   _____

6) _____   _____

7) _____   _____

8) _____   _____

9) _____   _____

10) _____   _____

11) _____   _____

12) _____   _____

GRAND TOTAL

STRATEGY: ANALYZING GROWTH PATTERNS

Here are two examples of growth patterns. Study these and use blocks and the Pattern Block template to create growth patterns of your own.

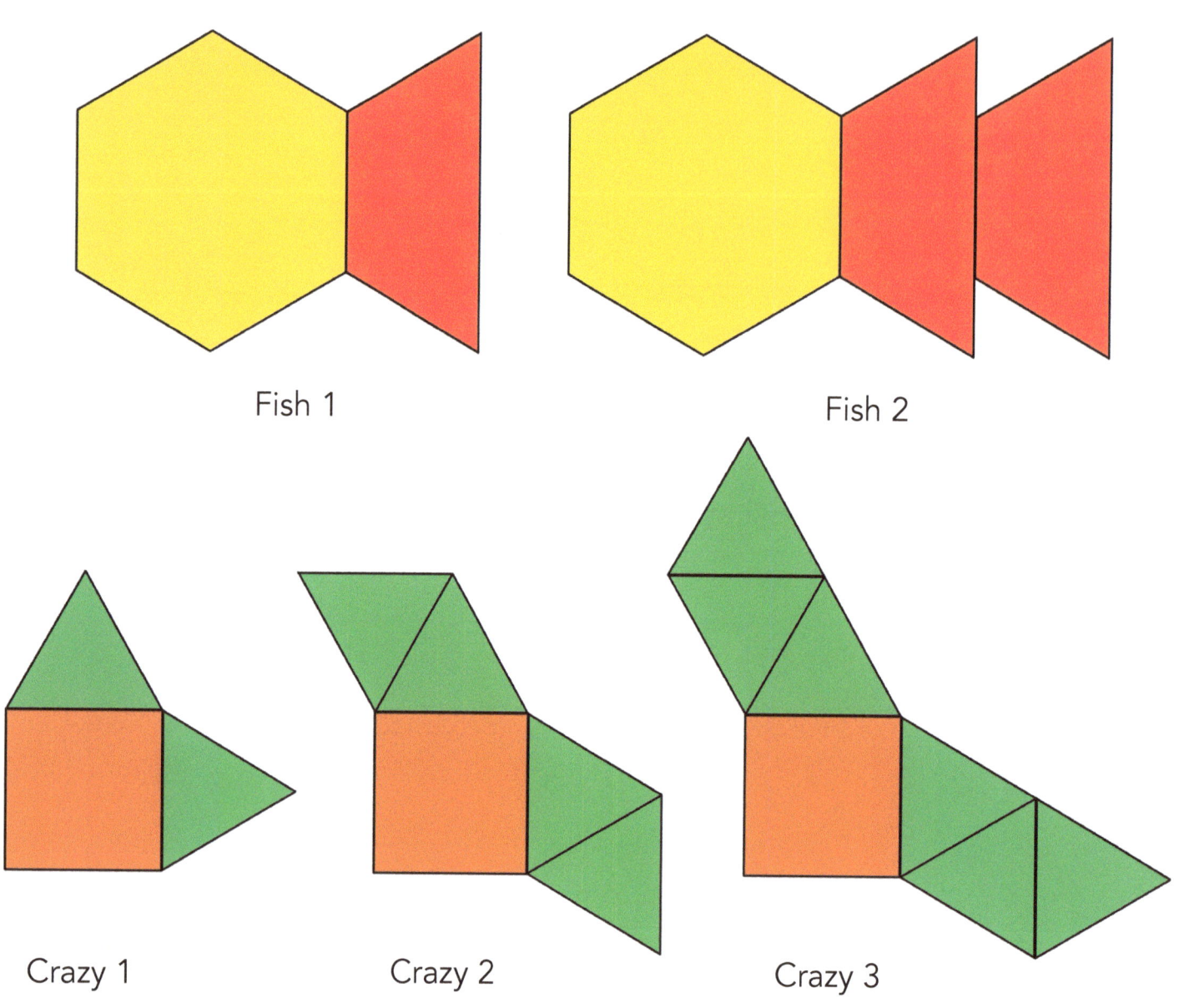

Fish 1

Fish 2

Crazy 1

Crazy 2

Crazy 3

Write a number pattern for your design like the two below:

Fish 1 = 2 Blocks, Fish 2 = 3 Blocks, so Fish 3 will equal 4 blocks, etc.

Crazy Creature 1 = 3 Blocks, Crazy Creature 2 = 5 Blocks, Crazy Creature 3 = 7 Blocks, so Crazy Creature 4 will equal 9 Blocks, and Crazy Creature 5 will equal 11 Blocks.

SQUARE NUMBER GROWTH PATTERN

How many orange squares fill each square below?

_____ Squares

_____ Squares

_____ Squares

_____ Squares

SQUARE NUMBER PATTERN
USING TRIANGLES

How many green triangles fill each triangle below?

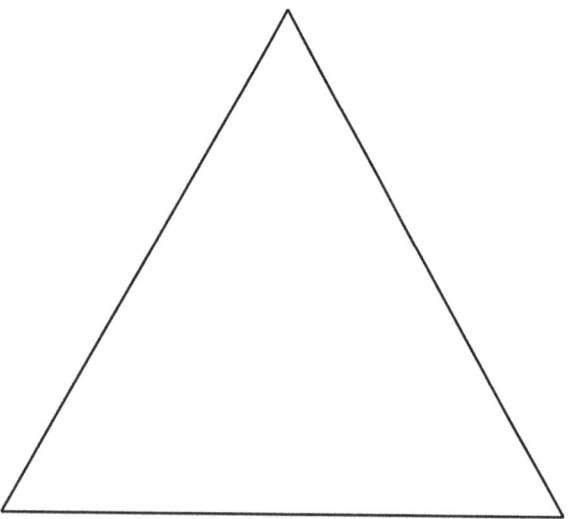

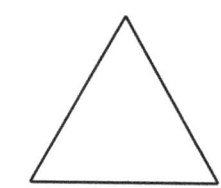

_____ Triangles

_____ Triangles

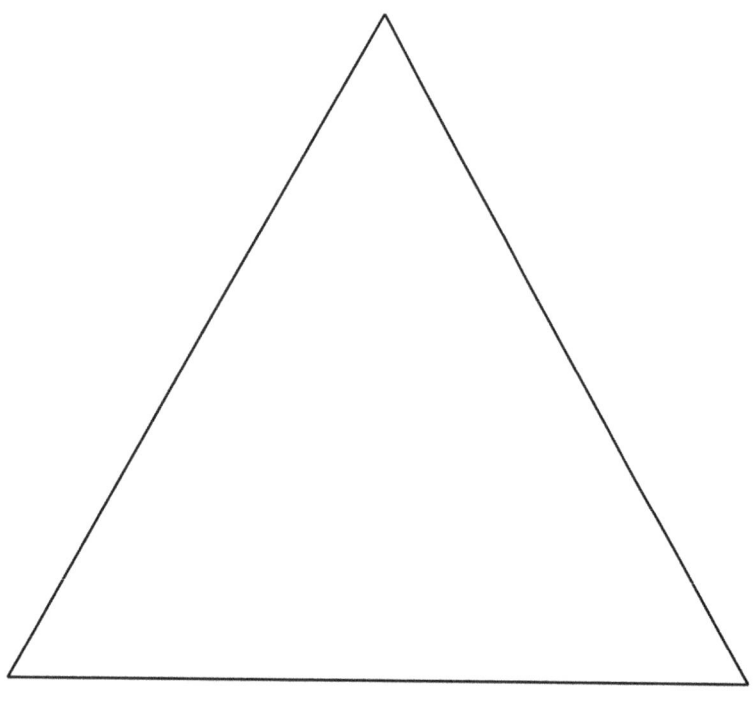

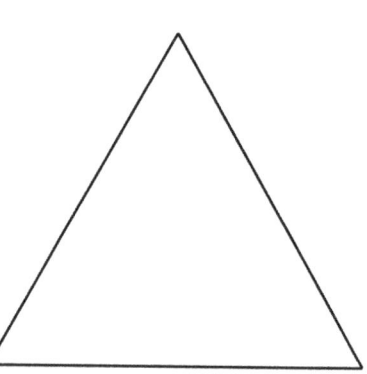

_____ Triangles

_____ Triangles

GROWTH PATTERN WITH TRIANGULAR NUMBERS

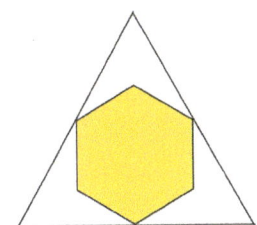

1 is the first triangular number

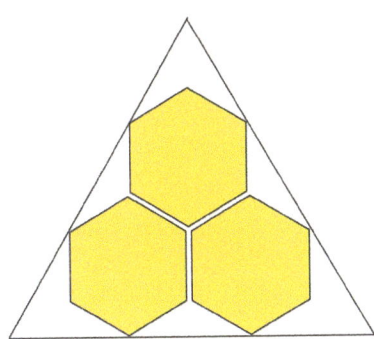

3 is the second triangular number

Does this look like bowling pins?

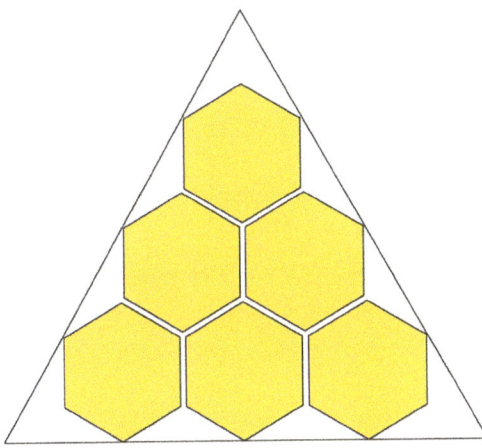

6 is the third triangular number

1) Using hexagons, see if you can make the fourth triangular number.

How many hexagons did you use? _____

2) What is the fifth triangular number? _____

3) Can you predict the eighth triangular number?

What is it? _____

2) What is the tenth triangular number? _____

GROWTH PATTERNS WITH HEXAGONAL NUMBERS

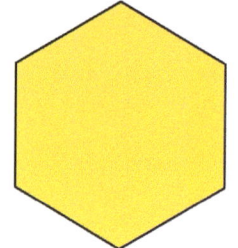

The first hexagonal number

The second hexagonal number

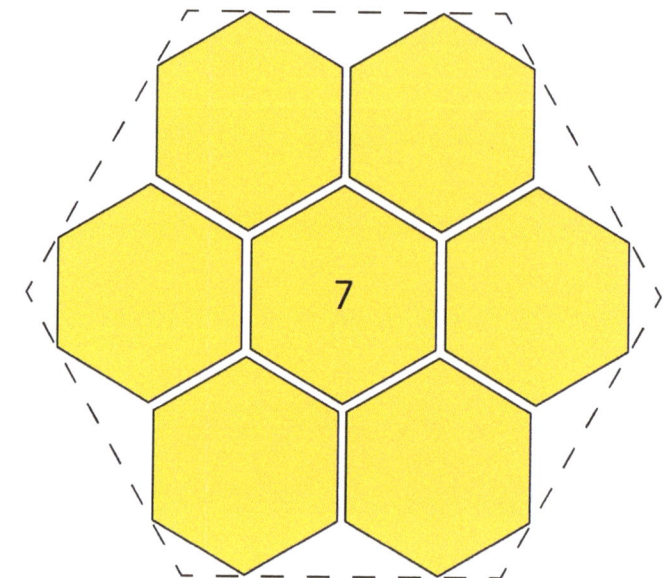

1) Can you make the third hexagonal number?

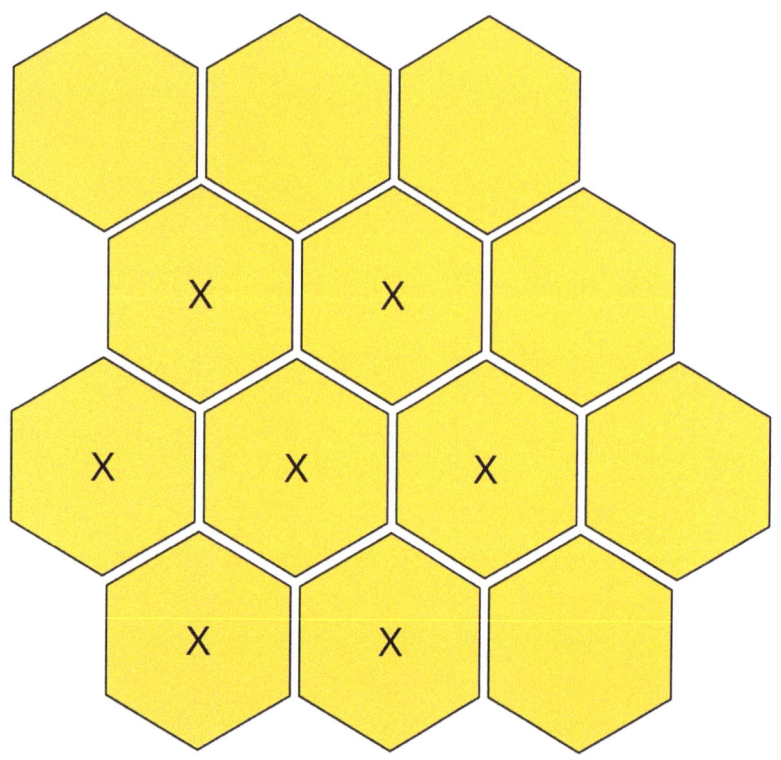

2) The fourth hexagonal Number is?

_____

How many hexagons did you use? _____

GROWTH PATTERN WITH 3 BLOCKS

Build a small animal using these shapes.

Draw your animal here:

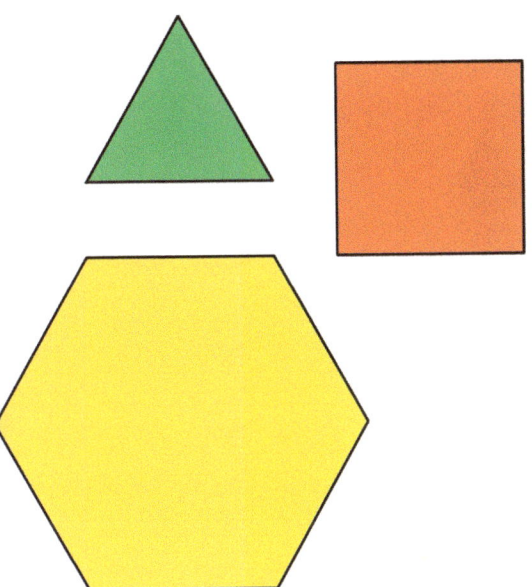

In the table below, enter the number of each kind of block you will need for more animals:

	Squares	Triangles	Hexagons
1 Animal			
2 Animals			
3 Animals			
5 Animals			
10 Animals			

FAIR TRADING WITH GROWTH PATTERNS

1. Fair trade: △ △ for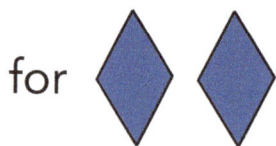

Trade   for ◆ ◆

Trade △ △ △ △ △ △ for

---

2. Fair trade: △ △ △ for ⬯

Trade   for ⬯ ⬯ ⬯ ⬯

---

3. Fair trade: ⬡ for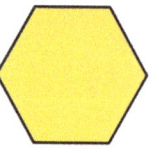

Trade   for

Trade ⬡ ⬡ ⬡ ⬡ for

GROWING A SHAPE FOR PROPORTIONAL REASONING

This activity builds understanding of algebraic sequences. Students will identify patterns of growth and describe rules for predicting the next output. They need to find the solution by building and counting. Then, they need to write a rule for future growth. Think about growth of an animal from year to year.

One example is the fish:

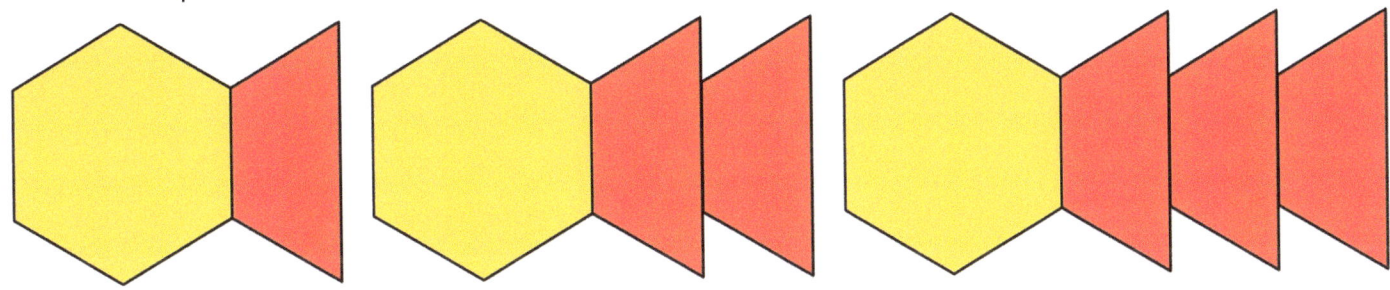

	Year 1	Year 2	Year 3	Year 4	Year 5
Number of Blocks	2	3	4		

The Rule: Year number plus 1

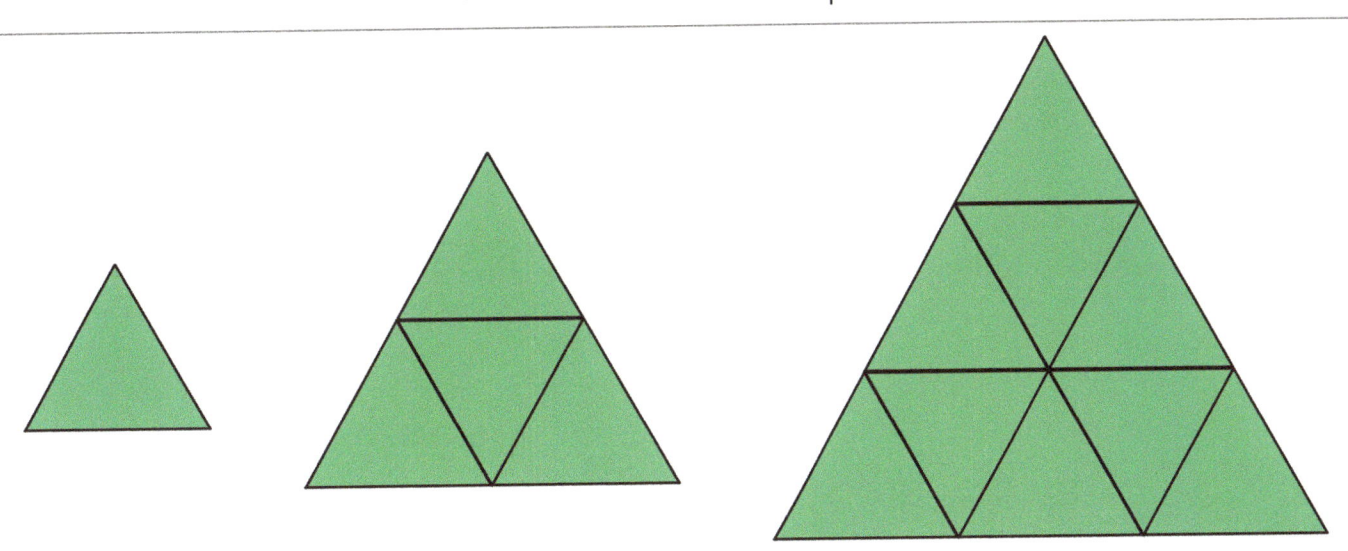

	Year 1	Year 2	Year 3	Year 4	Year 5
Number of Blocks	1	4	9		

The Rule: Year number times year number

PROPORTIONAL REASONING PATTERNS

IN	OUT
1	2
2	4
	6
	14
9	
	38

What is the rule?

_____

_____

_____

IN	OUT
1	6
2	11
3	16
4	
9	
	51

What is the rule?

_____

_____

_____

IN	OUT
0	
1	3
2	5
3	
4	

What is the rule?

_____

_____

_____

DIRECTIONS FOR MIRROR AND ROTATIONAL SYMMETRY

Investigations with symmetry develop spatial reasoning abilities. Neurological research supports that visual tasks enhance verbal, logical, and sequential processing skills. Students enjoy building symmetrical models and naturally create designs with a variety of symmetrical elements.

Mirror Symmetry

Begin by drawing images that will be seen two different ways if you place a mirror in the middle. For example, draw a dish and put food only on one side. Now, you see two different images when you look at both sides of the mirror. One image is a full plate, and the other is an empty plate.

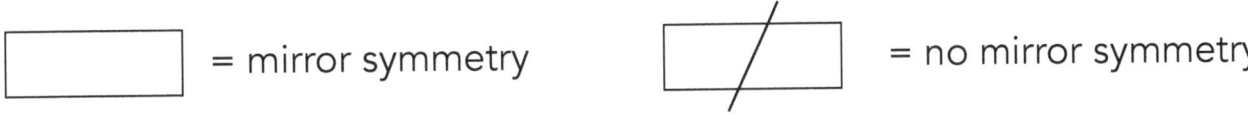

Rotational Symmetry

This section is primarily for children 7 and older. Mirror symmetry makes sense to young learners, but they often build designs that have rotational symmetry. Turning shapes can be accomplished by building on a cardboard and then turning the cardboard to a new position. To test rotational symmetry, place the blocks on cardboard, then turn the cardboard to a new position. The slash through the rotational symmetry symbol indicates there is no rotational symmetry.

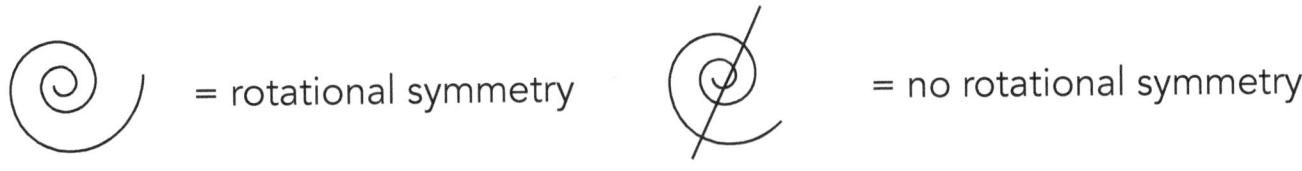

Both Mirror and Rotational Symmetry

Investigate capital letters of the alphabet. Which ones have mirror symmetry, and which ones have rotational symmetry? Which letters have both?

USE SIMPLE MIRROR

What do you see?

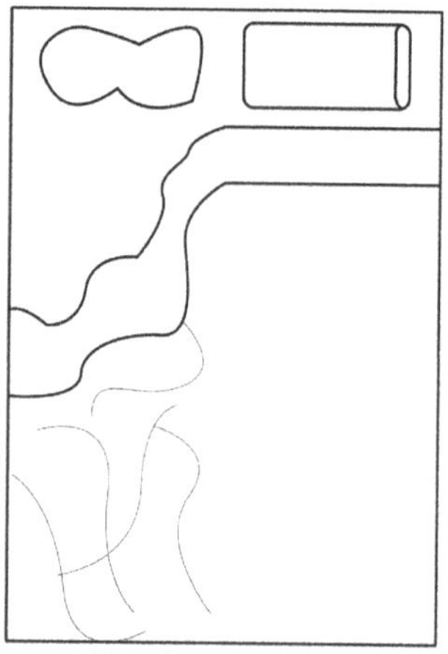

Messy Bed   Neat Bed

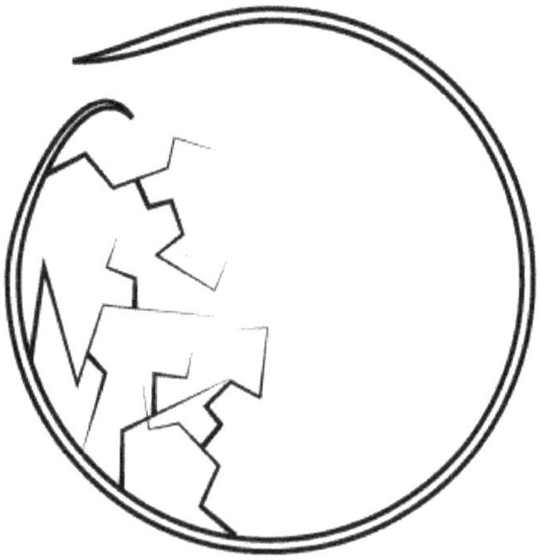

Cracked   New

Try making your own!

Counting: How many people can you see?

Move the mirror around and circle the number!

1   2   3   4

5   6   7   8

MIRROR SYMMETRY

Mirror Images

Build the other side of the image.
Draw what you see with Pattern Block template.

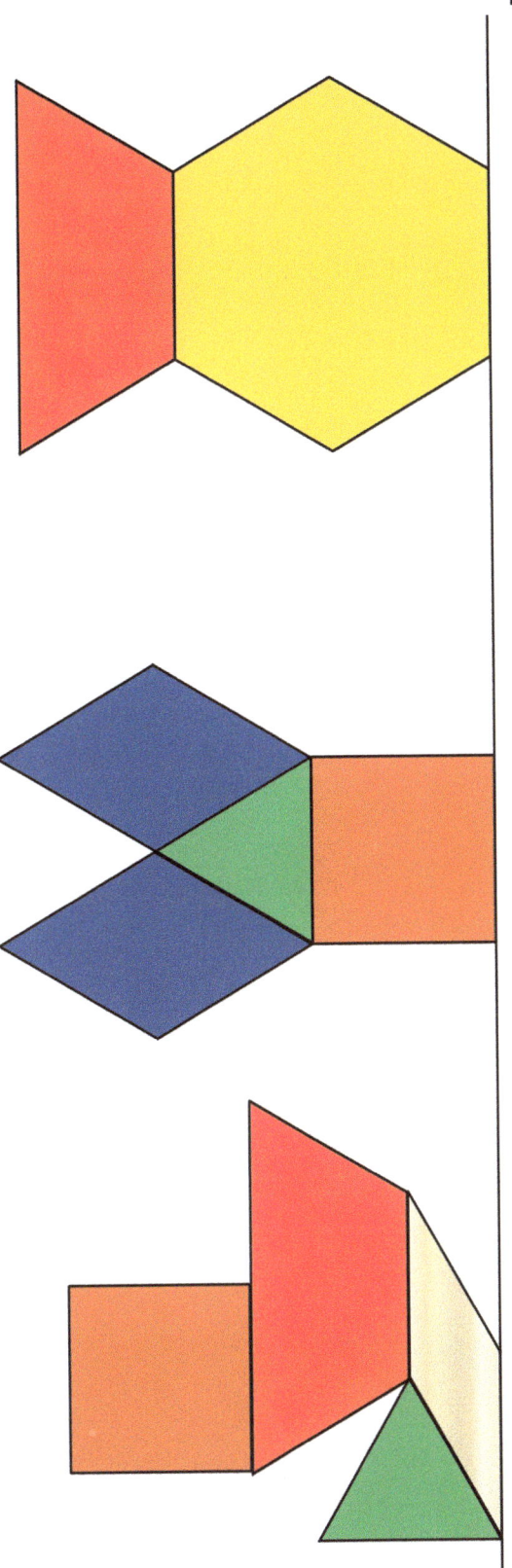

MORE MIRROR SYMMETRY:
Use a mirror and template to draw mirror images.

For fun, create a butterfly or other animal with mirror symmetry.

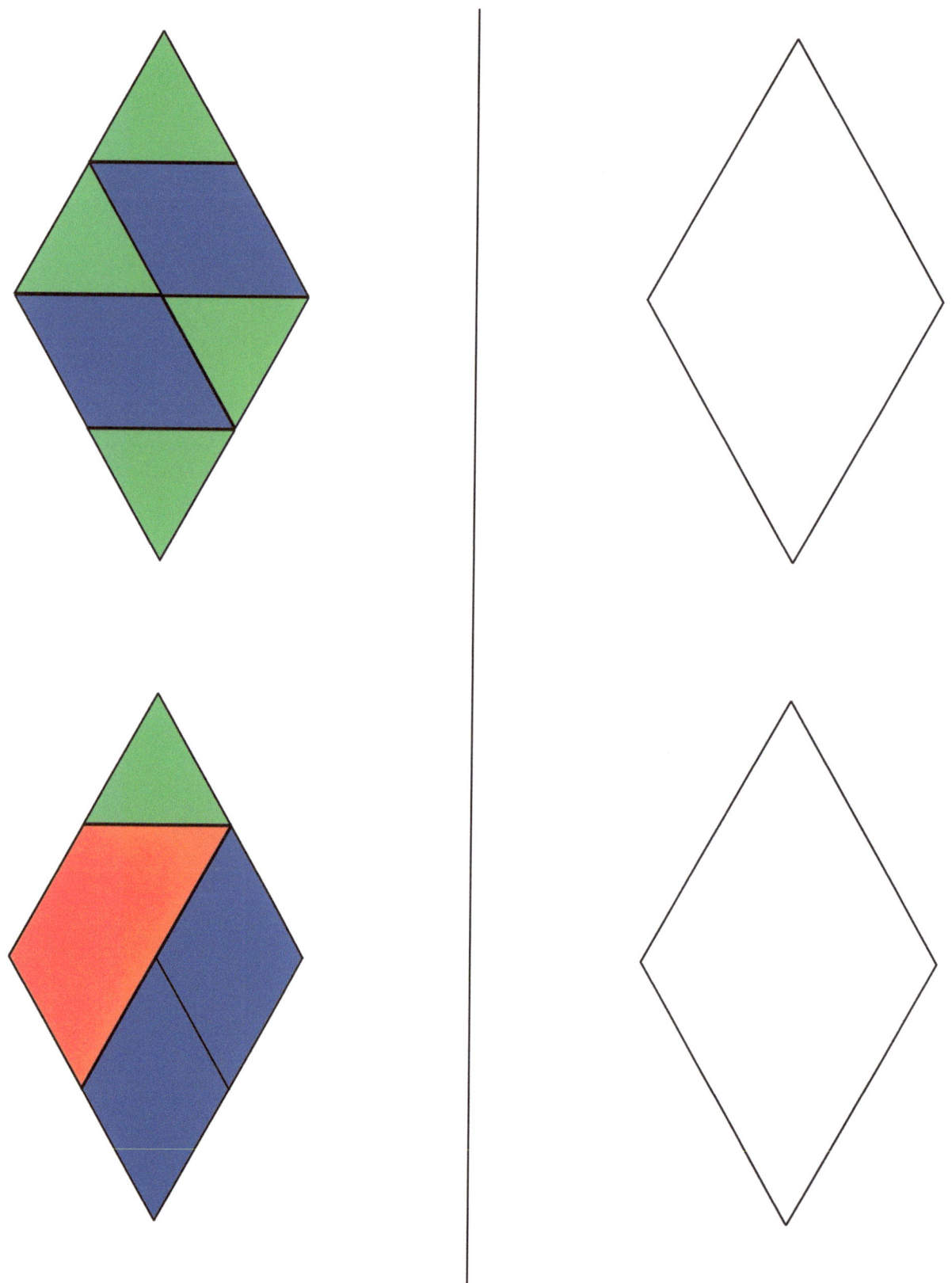

EVEN MORE MIRROR SYMMETRY:
Use a mirror and template to draw mirror images.

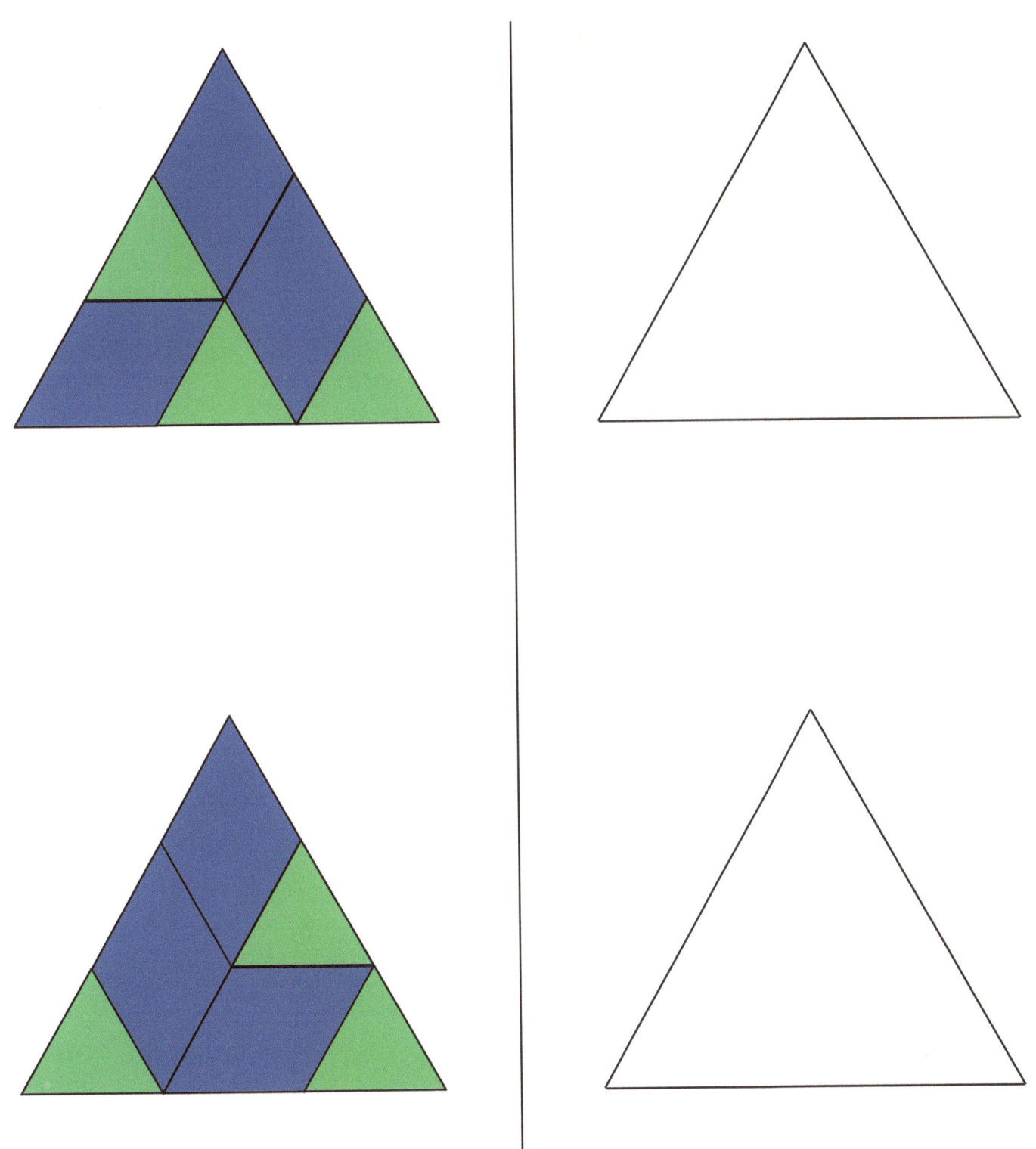

MIRROR SYMMETRY - TRAPEZOID

Do these shapes have mirror symmetry?
Place mirror on the arrows. Circle correct answer.

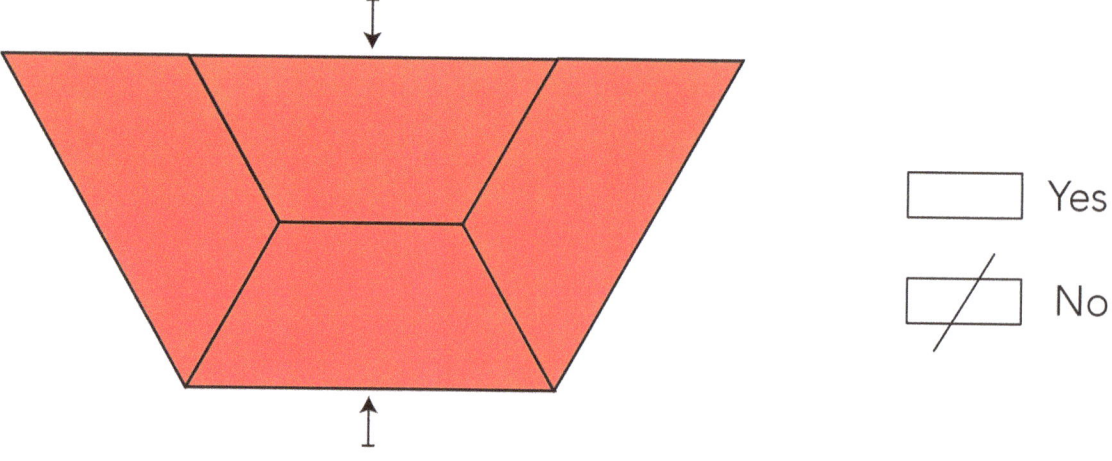

Yes

No

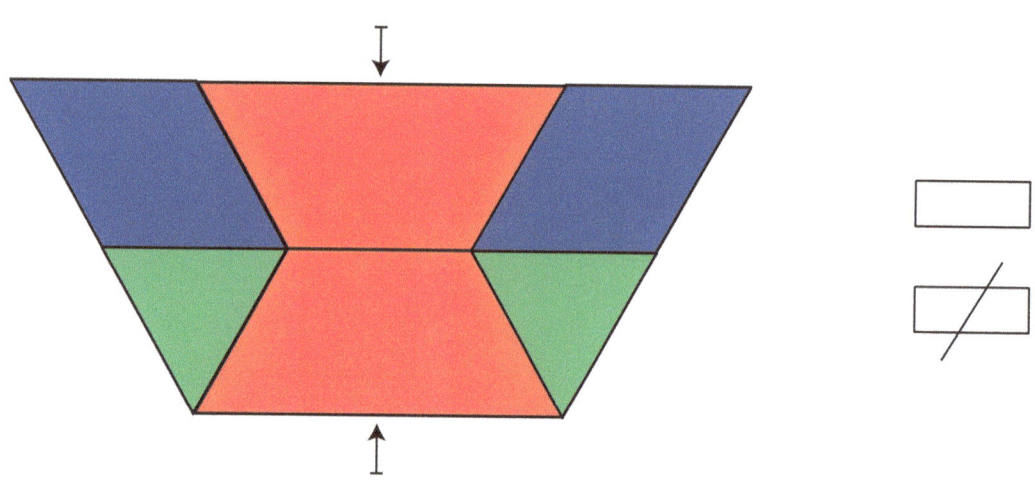

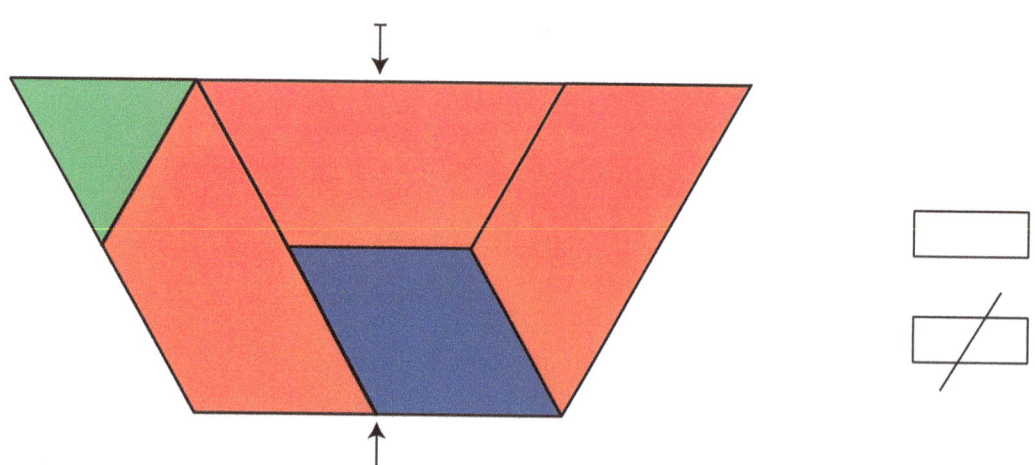

MIRROR SYMMETRY - MORE TRAPEZOIDS

Do these shapes have mirror symmetry?
Place mirror on arrows. Circle correct answer.

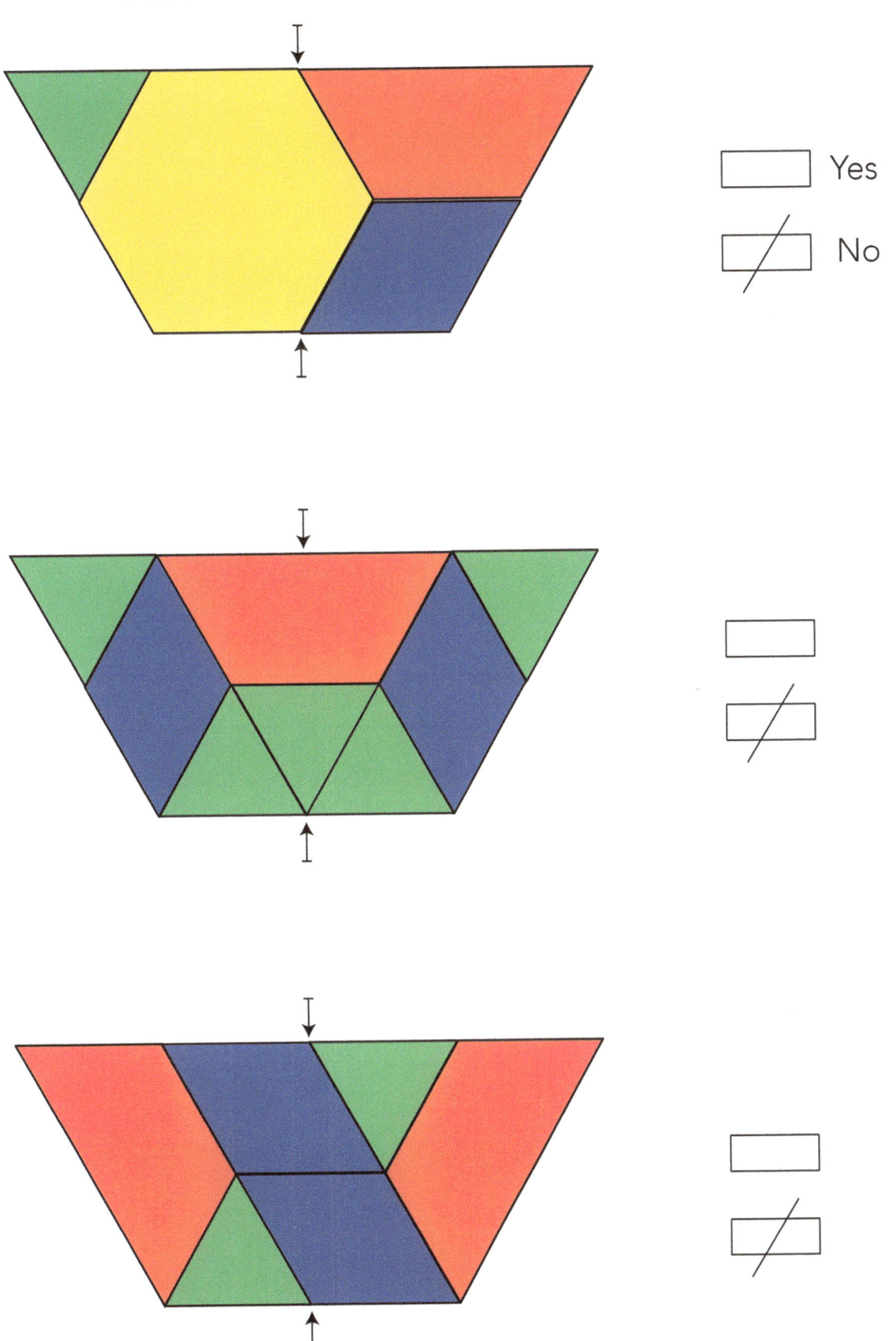

Yes

No

MIRROR SYMMETRY - RHOMBUS

Do these shapes have mirror symmetry?
Place mirror on the arrows. Circle correct answer.

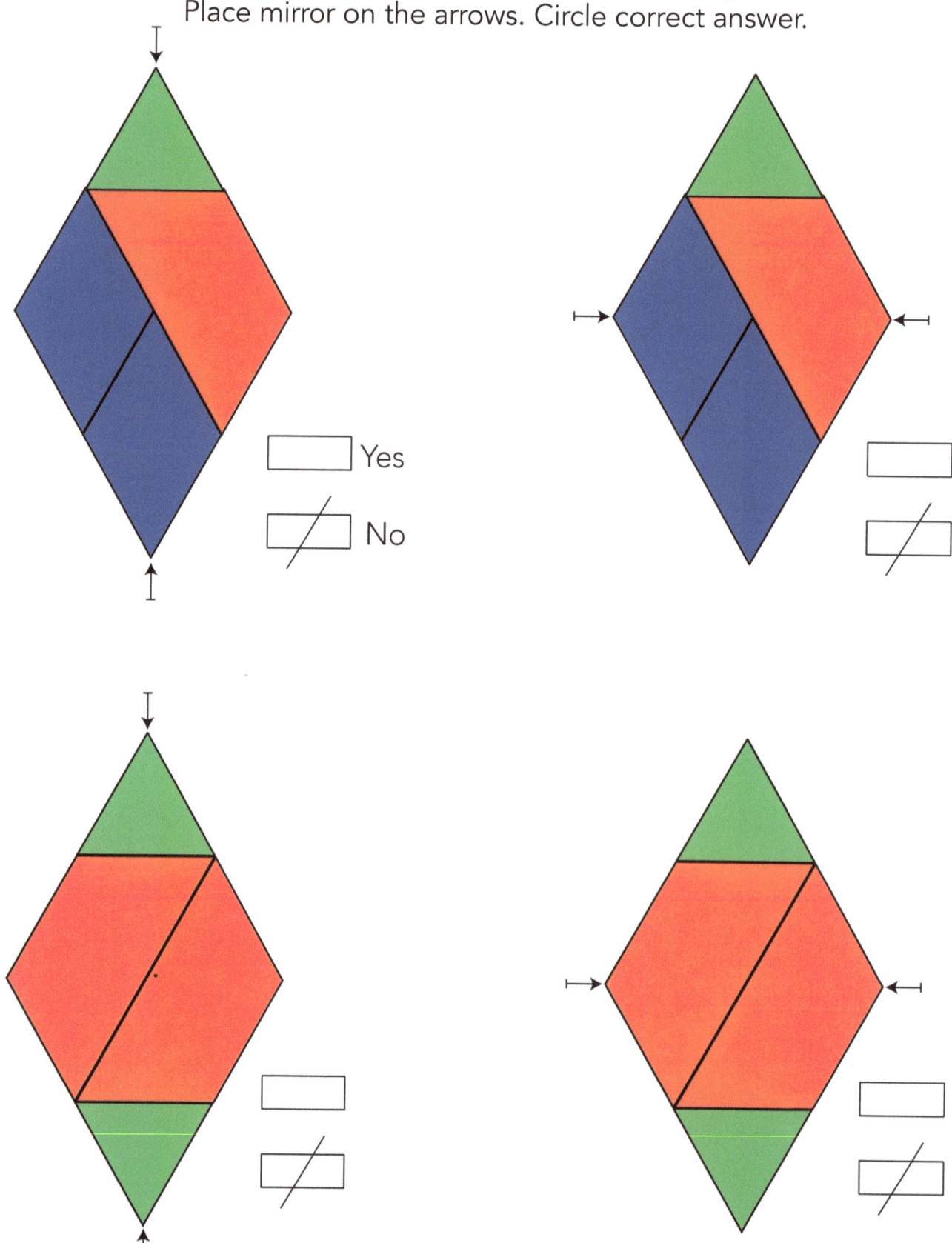

Yes

No

MIRROR SYMMETRY - HEXAGON

Do these shapes have mirror symmetry?
Place mirror on the arrows. Circle correct answer.

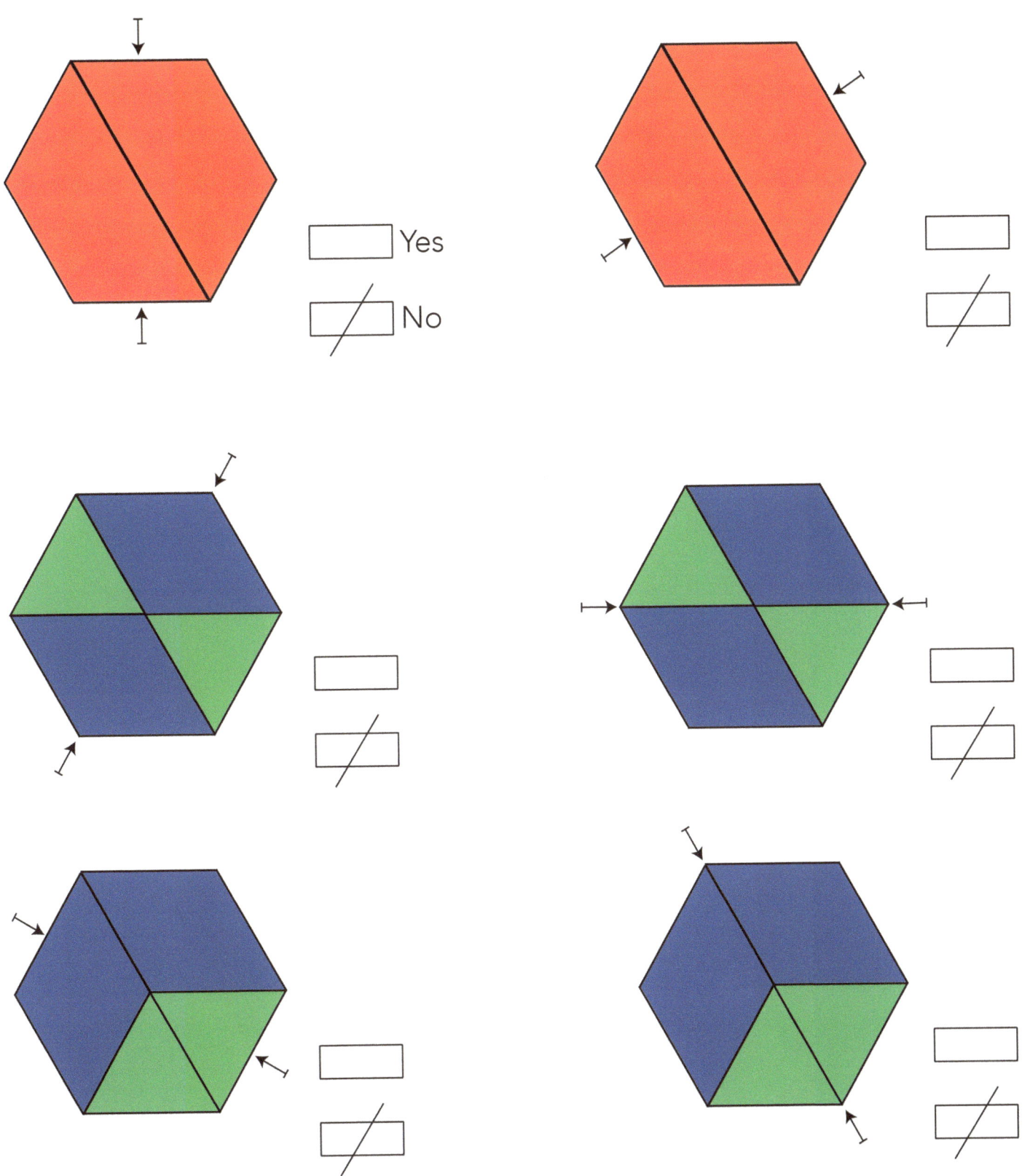

Yes

No

ROTATIONAL SYMMETRY - RHOMBUS

Do these shapes have rotational symmetry?
Build each shape on an index card. Rotate it in a circle. If the shape is identical to the beginning shape at least once before the card is turned all the way around, the shape has rotational symmetry.

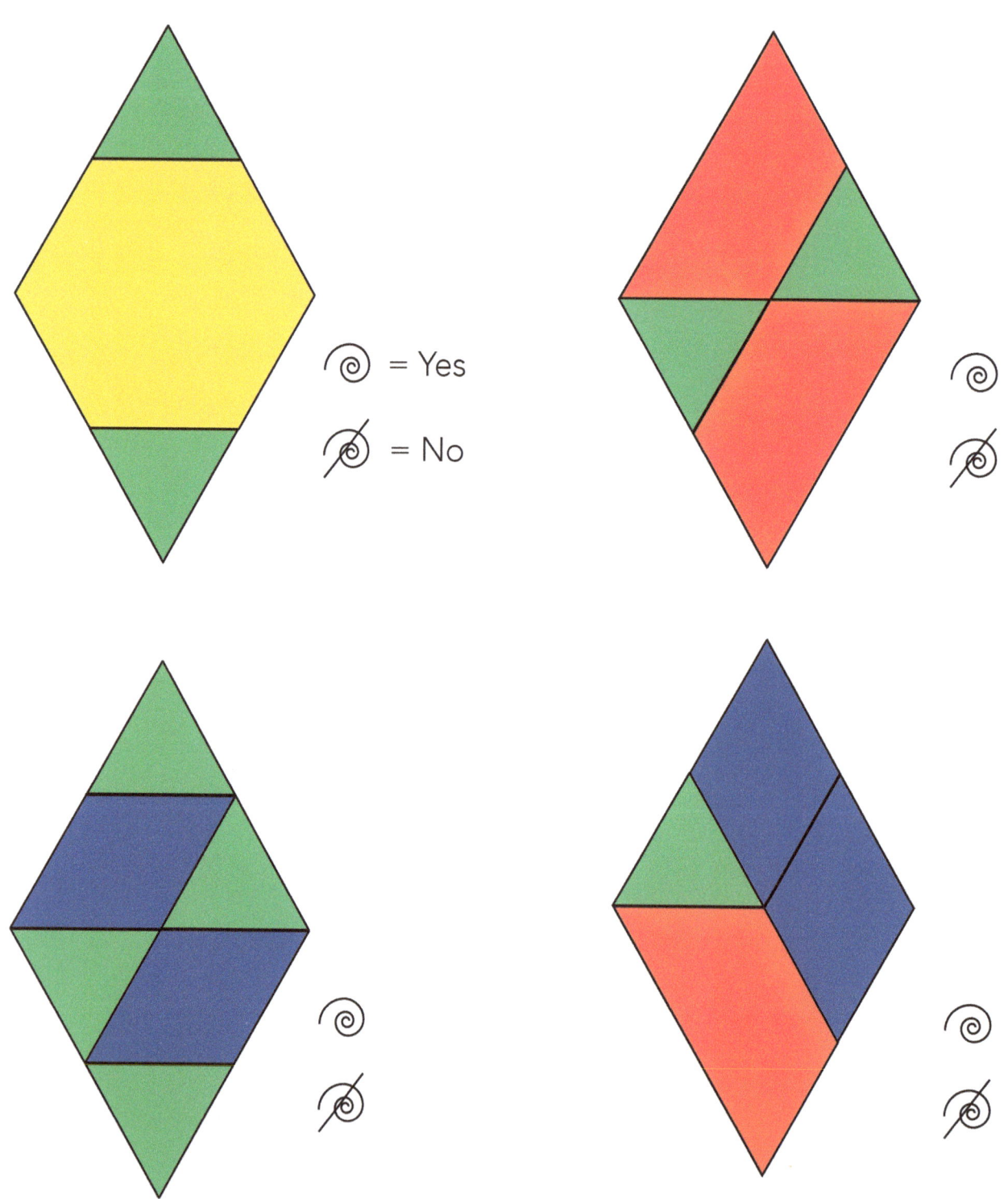

= Yes

= No

ROTATIONAL SYMMETRY - STARS

Do these shapes have rotational symmetry?
Circle the correct answer.

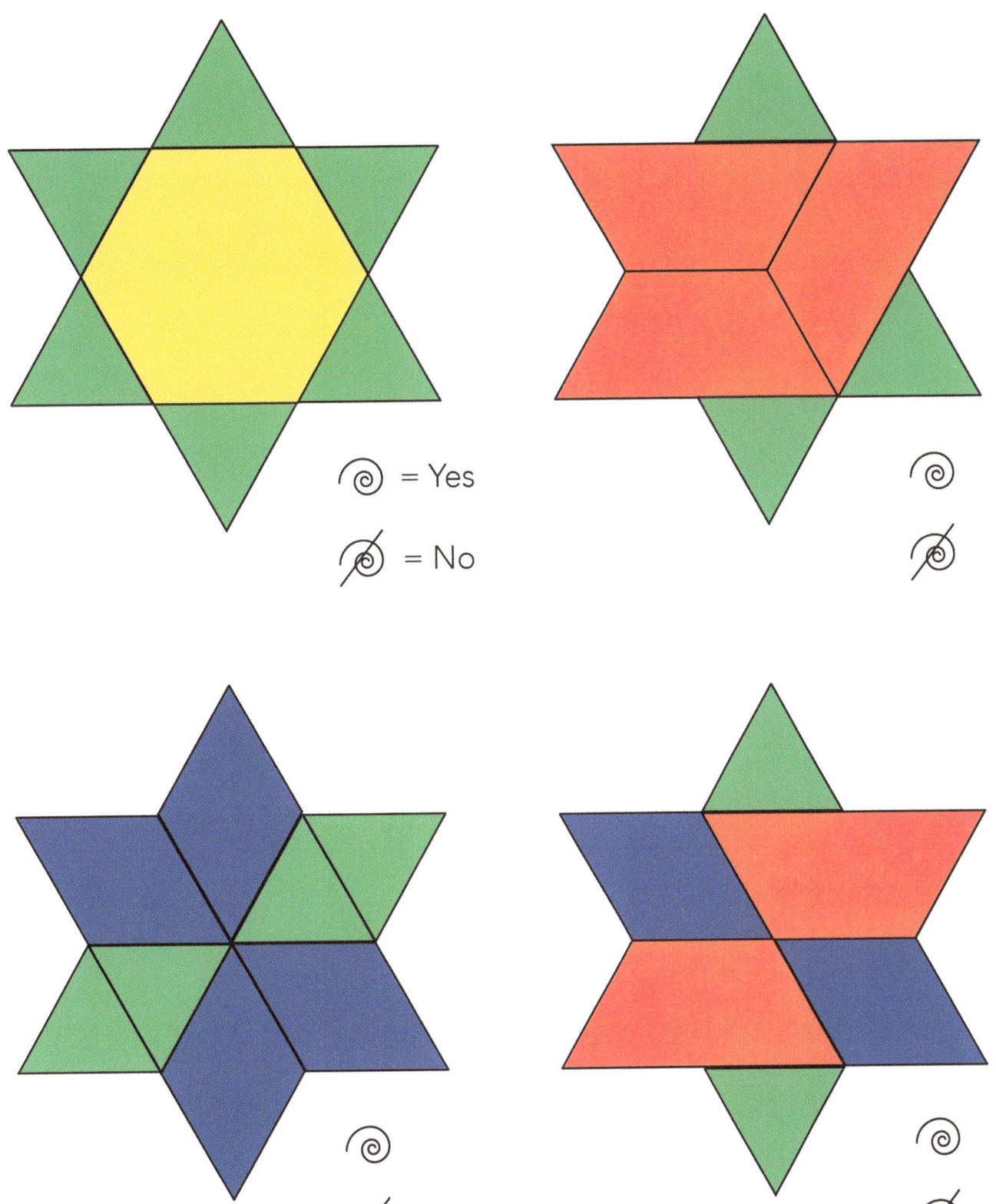

◉ = Yes

∅ = No

ROTATIONAL SYMMETRY - TRIANGLE

Do these shapes have rotational symmetry?
Circle the correct answer.

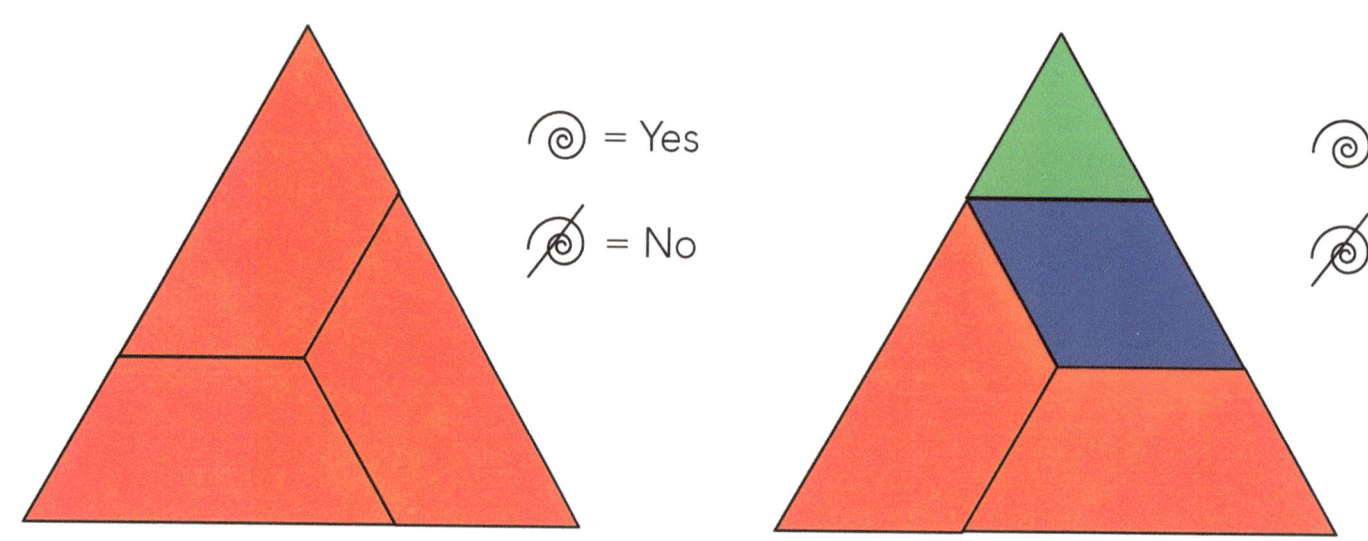

= Yes

= No

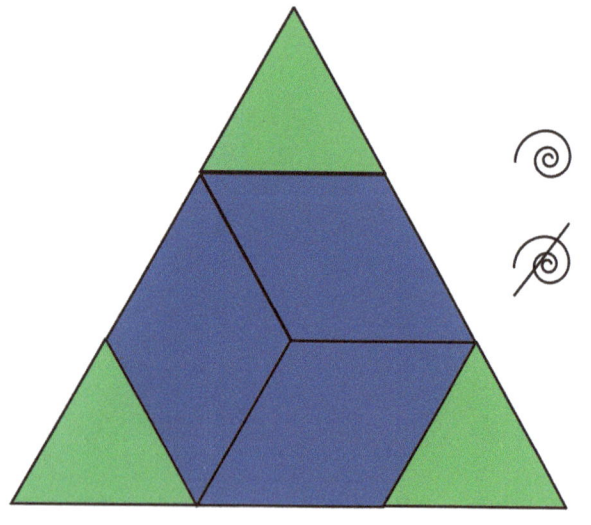

BOTH SYMMETRIES

Make all of the triangles below with 3 blue Pattern Blocks and 3 green Pattern Blocks. Follow the instructions below each shape for the symmetry rules.

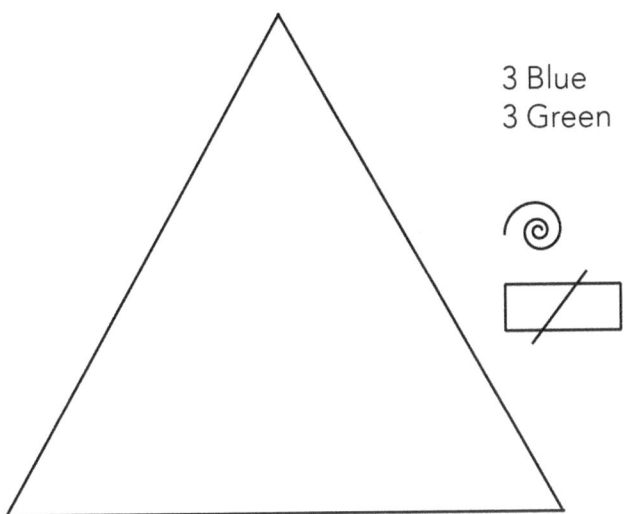

3 Blue
3 Green

Shape must have rotational symmetry.
Shape cannot have mirror symmetry.

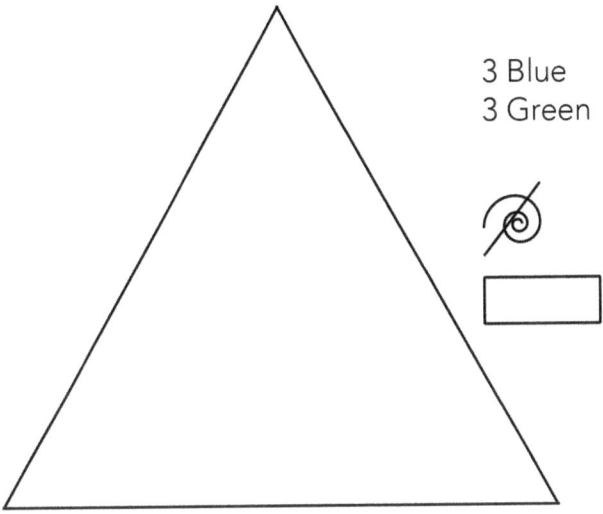

3 Blue
3 Green

Shape cannot have rotational symmetry.
Shape must have mirror symmetry.

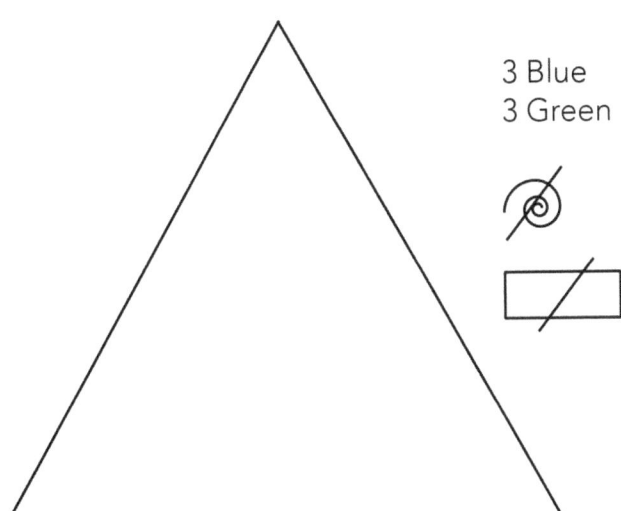

3 Blue
3 Green

Shape cannot have rotational symmetry.
Shape cannot have mirror symmetry.

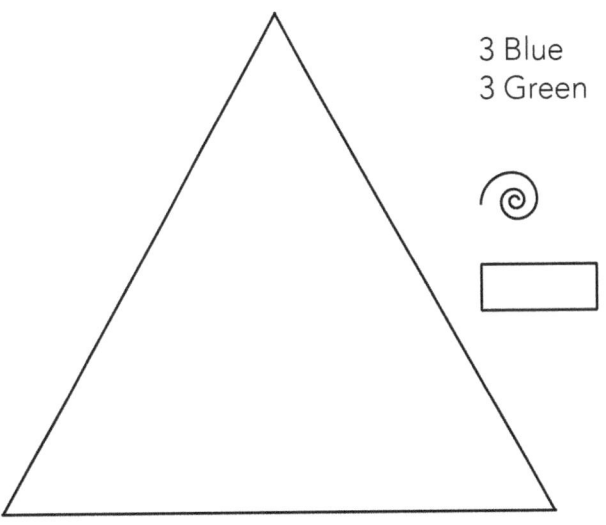

3 Blue
3 Green

Shape must have rotational symmetry.
Shape must have mirror symmetry.

MORE PRACTICE FOR BOTH SYMMETRIES

Follow the instructions next to each shape for the Pattern Block and symmetry rules.

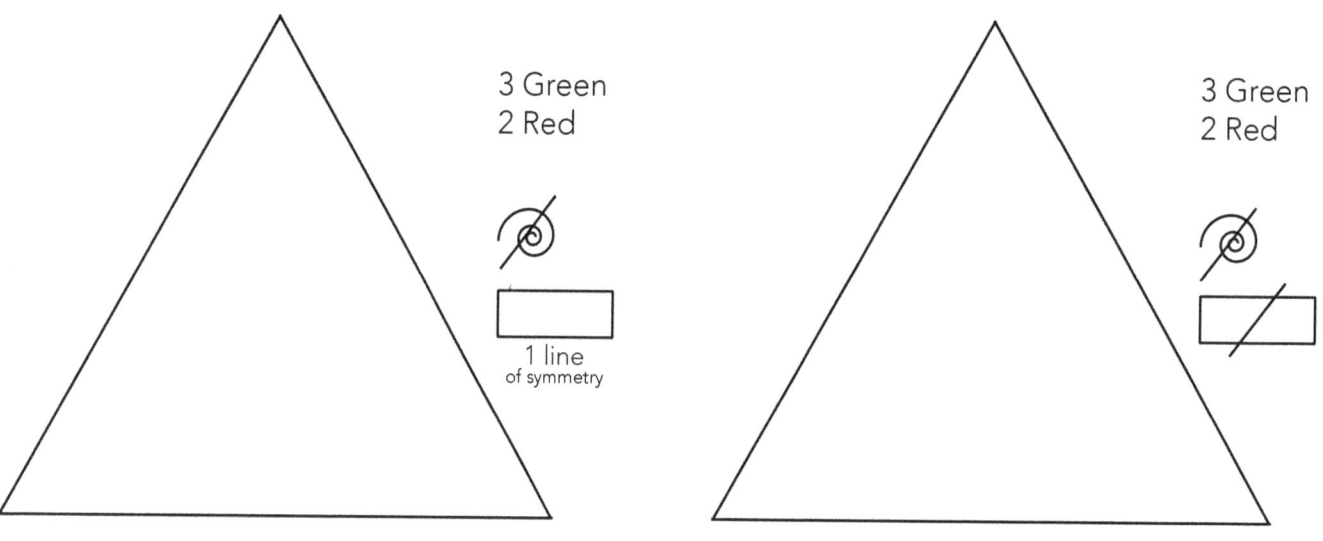

3 Green
2 Red

1 line
of symmetry

3 Green
2 Red

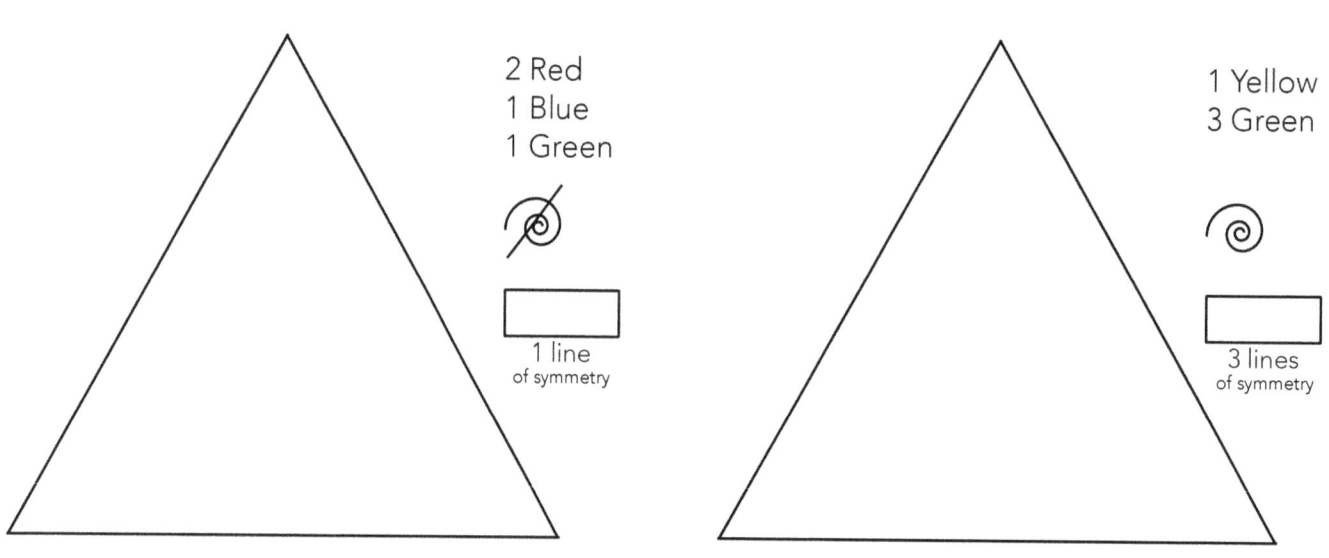

2 Red
1 Blue
1 Green

1 line
of symmetry

1 Yellow
3 Green

3 lines
of symmetry

For fun create an animal or different shape with rotational symmetry!

OCTAGON SYMMETRY

Fill the two octagons with Pattern Blocks
One should have mirror symmetry and the other one should not.

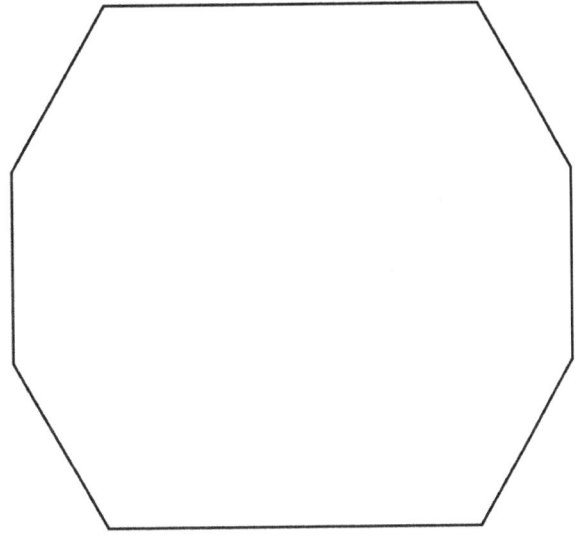

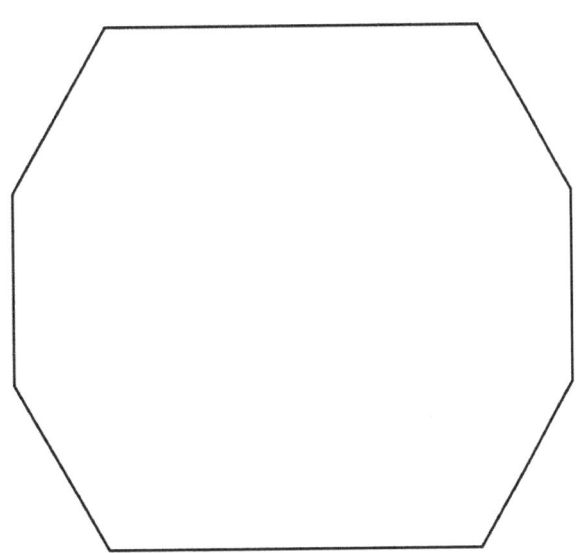

HEXAGON SYMMETRY

Fill the three hexagons with Pattern Blocks.
One has mirror symmetry, one should have rotational symmetry, and one should have both.

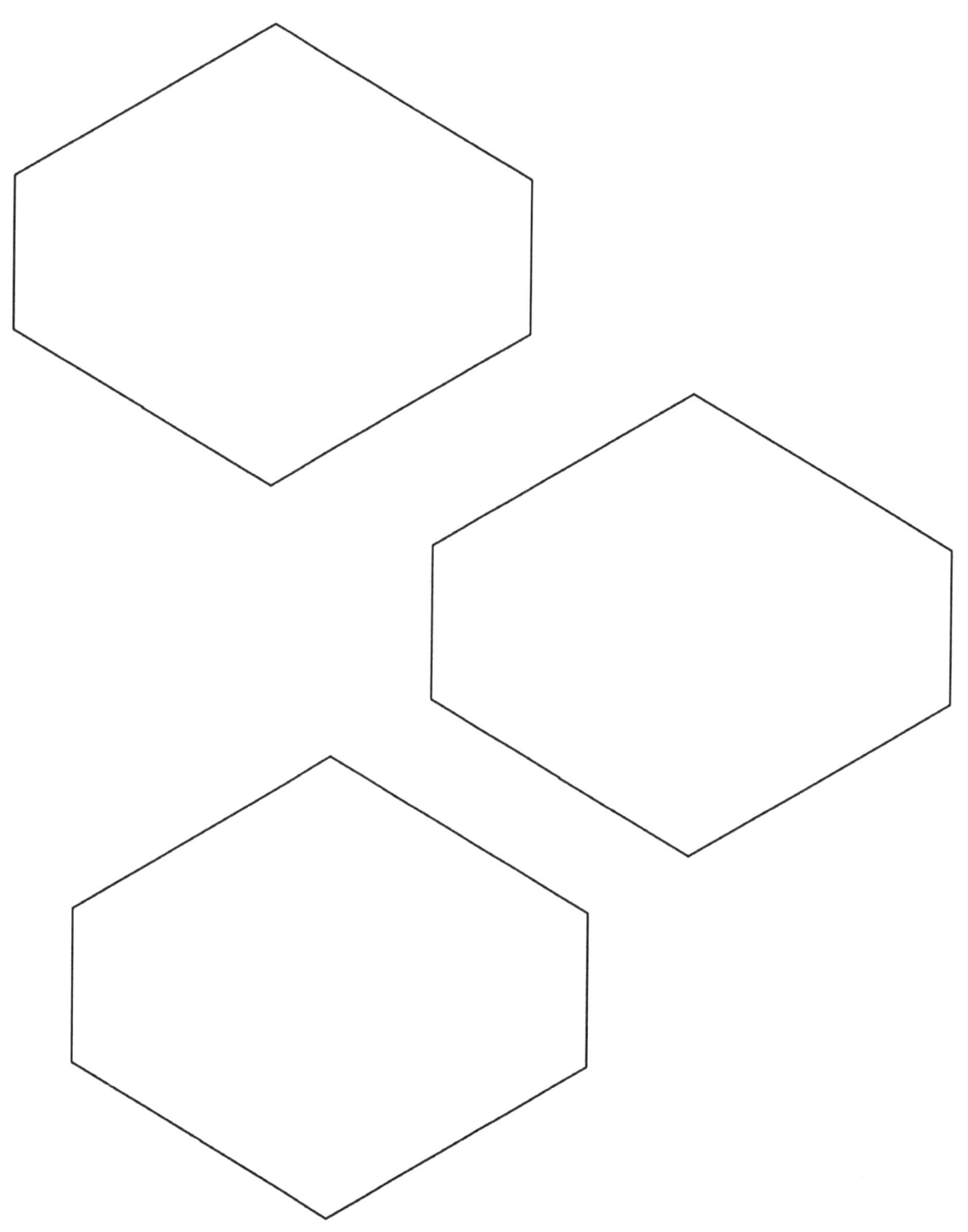

THE DODECAGON

The **dodecagon** can be filled with Pattern Blocks hundreds of different ways. In fact, there are so many ways that there are rules to limit the number of ways.

Rule 1: Two adjacent triangles must be replaced with a blue rhombus.

Rule 2: An adjacent triangle and blue rhombus must be replaced with a trapezoid.

Rule 3: Three adjacent blue rhombuses must be replaced with a yellow hexagon.

Rule 4: Two adjacent trapezoids must be replaced with a hexagon.

Once a new dodecagon design is created, it is to be drawn and colored using the Pattern Block template.

On the next page, cut out the dodecagon along the edges and collect all the different dodecagons in an organized way either posted on a wall or in a booklet. There are four different types of dodecagons: those with mirror symmetry, rotational symmetry, both symmetries, and asymmetrical. If posting the cut-out dodecagons on a wall, create a Venn Diagram to organize them.

Basic Dodecagon:

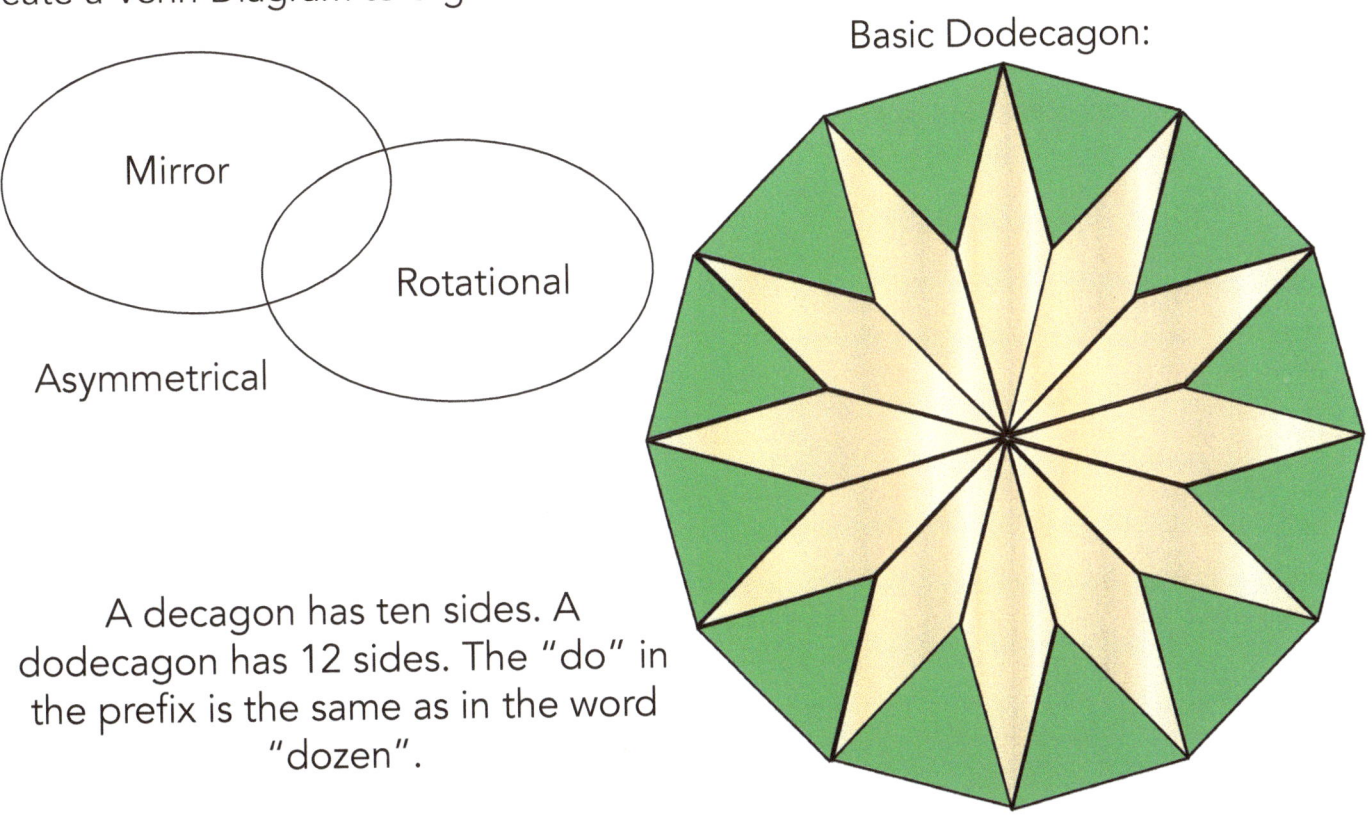

A decagon has ten sides. A dodecagon has 12 sides. The "do" in the prefix is the same as in the word "dozen".

DODECAGON TEMPLATE
CREATE YOUR OWN EXAMPLES

MEASURING ANGLES

Two Mirror Exploration #1

1. Place hinged double mirror on the lines.
2. Place one Pattern Block near the mirror.
3. Then place two, three, four Pattern Blocks near the mirror.
4. Place any object near the mirror - pencil, scissors, pen, etc.
5. Record your favorite Pattern Block image with the Pattern Block template.

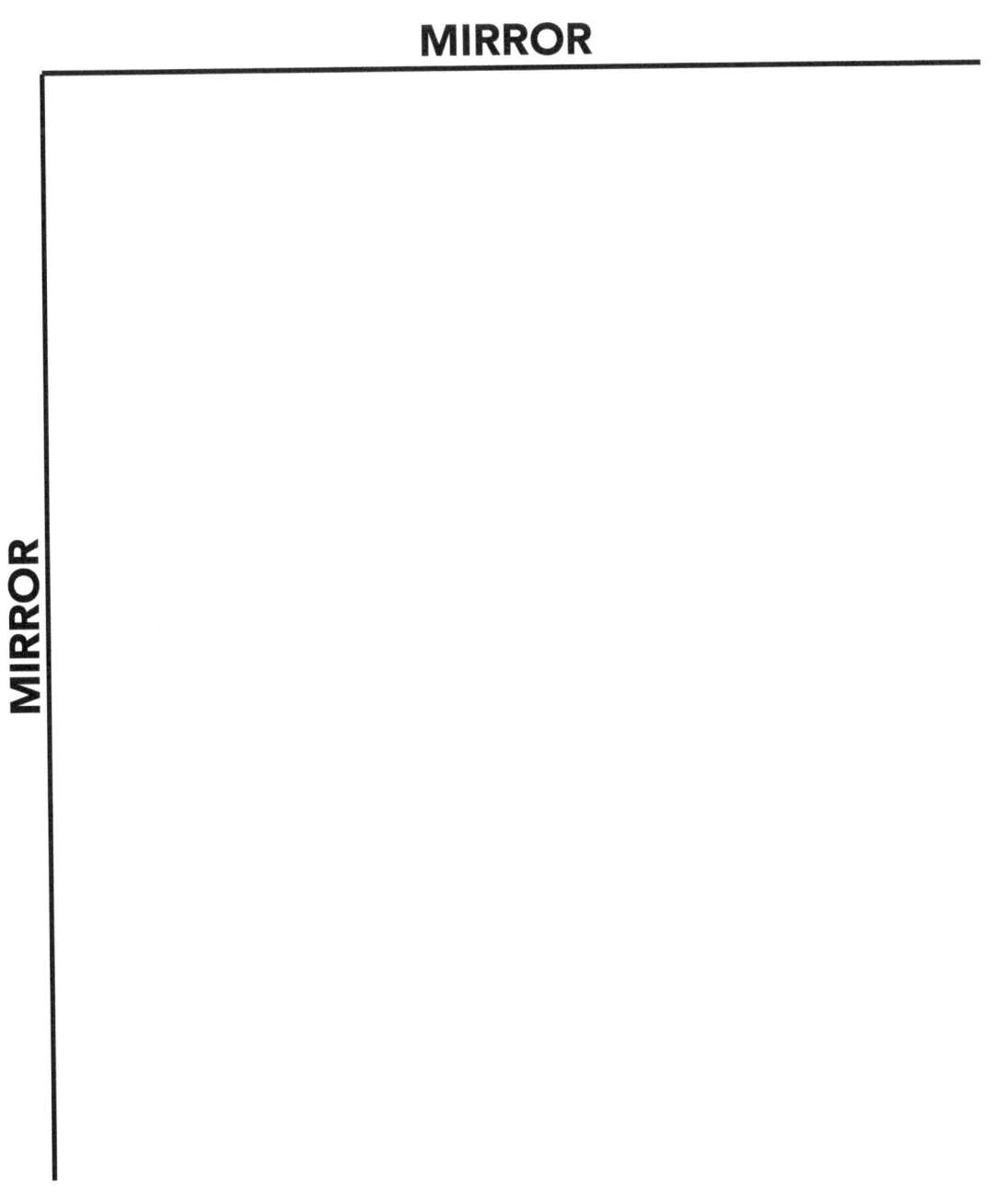

MIRROR

MIRROR

MEASURING ANGLES

Two Mirror Exploration #2

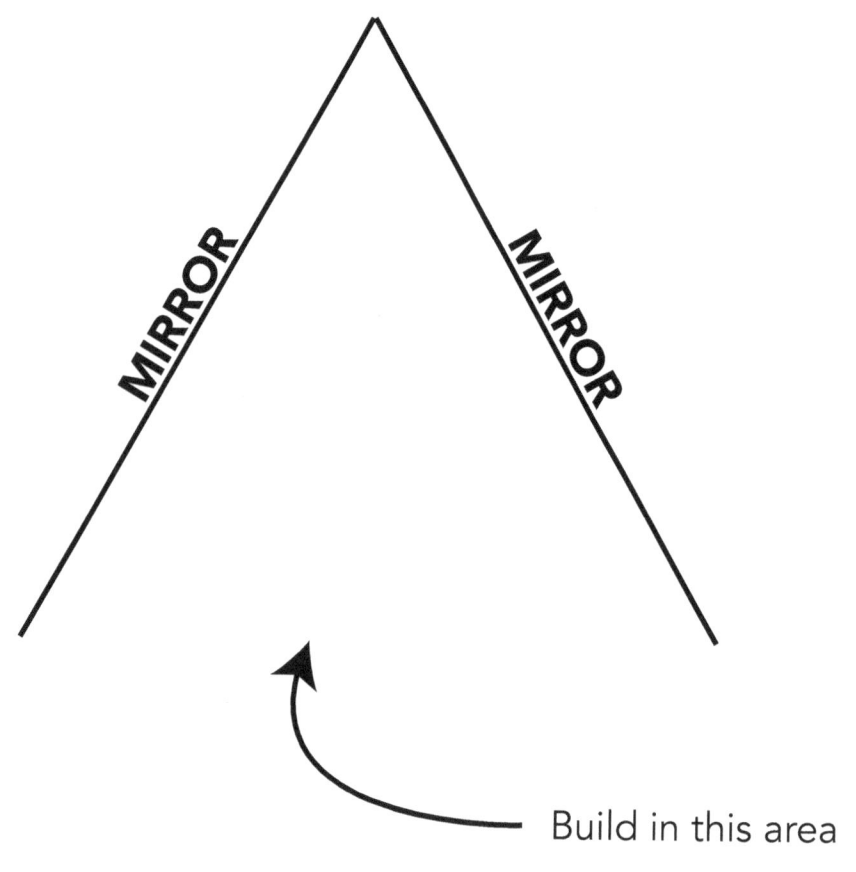

Build in this area

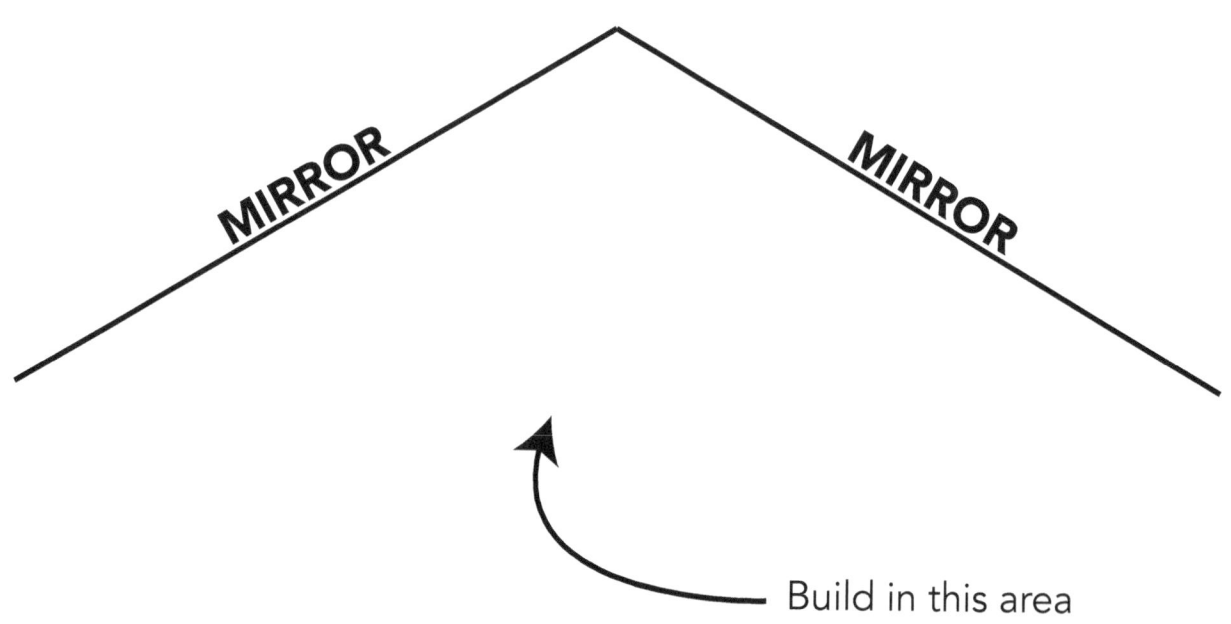

Build in this area

MEASURING ANGLES

Two Mirror Exploration #3

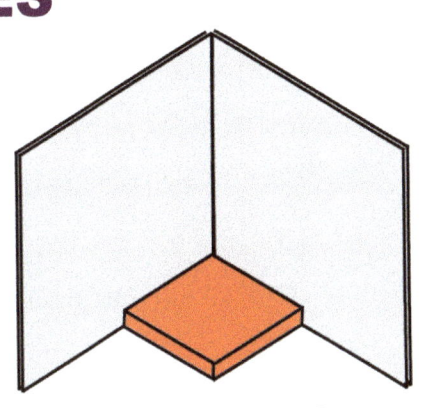

Use a hinged double mirror to wrap
around each Pattern Block.

Use Pattern Blocks to make an angle. How many blocks do you see?

Angle   Number of blocks in mirror

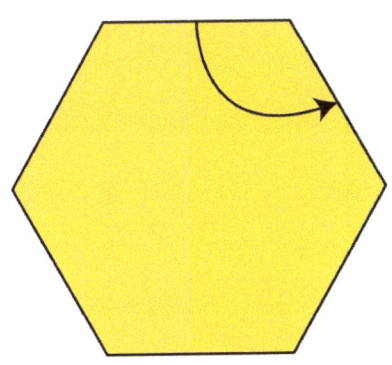

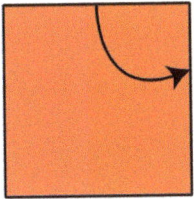

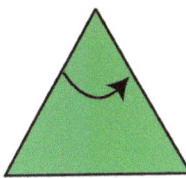

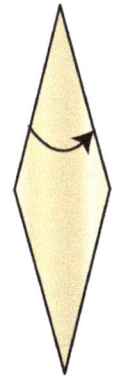

What rule can you make about this?

MEASURING ANGLES

Two Mirror Exploration #4

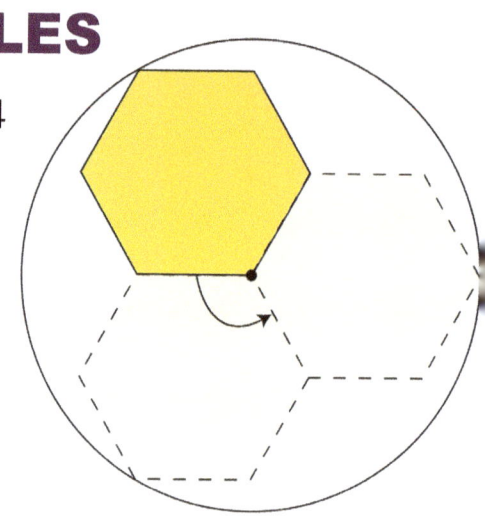

- There are 360° in a circle.
- Draw a dot. Put the corner of a Pattern Block on the dot.
- How many of the same block does it take to go around the dot?
- To find the size of the angle, divide 360° by the number of blocks it took.

Block Used	Times around	Problem	Size of angle
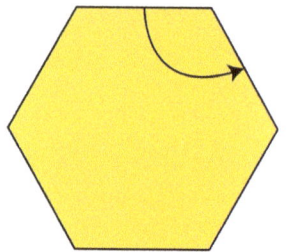	3	360 ÷ 3 =	_____
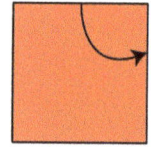		360 ÷ ____ =	_____
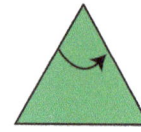		360 ÷ ____ =	_____
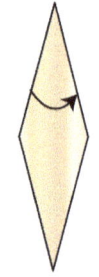		360 ÷ ____ =	_____
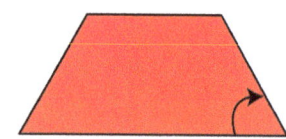		360 ÷ ____ =	_____

Use this method to name the size of other angles found on Tangrams, Geoblocks, Paper Triangles, or angles that you draw.

MEASURING ANGLES

Two Mirror Exploration #5

Finding angles with more than one block.

<u>Block Used</u>	<u>Times around</u>	<u>Problem</u>	<u>Size of angle</u>

  _____ $360 \div$ ____ = _____

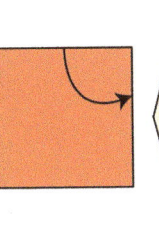  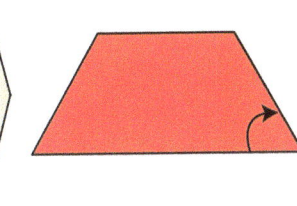 _____ $360 \div$ ____ = _____

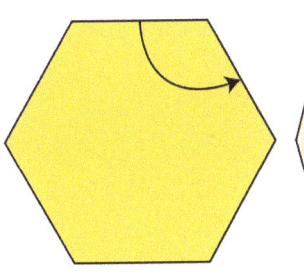 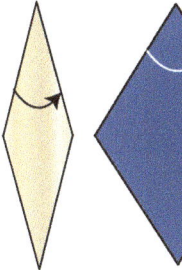 _____ $360 \div$ ____ = _____

Create your own:

MEASURING ANGLES
Two Mirror Exploration #6

- Using a hinged mirror, place the hinge on the dot.
- Change the angle between the mirrors until you see one of the shapes below.
- Mark the position of the mirrors.

Use a different color for each shape!

	Number of Sides	Name of Polygon	Color
	3	Triangle	_____
	4	Square	_____
	5	Pentagon	_____
	6	Hexagon	_____
	7	Heptagon	_____
	8	*Octagon	_____
	9	*Nonagon	_____
	10	*Decagon	_____
	12	*Dodecagon	_____

*Tricky!

MEASUREMENT: AREA

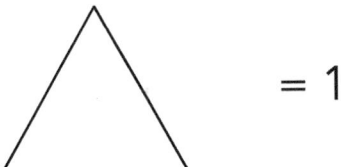 = 1

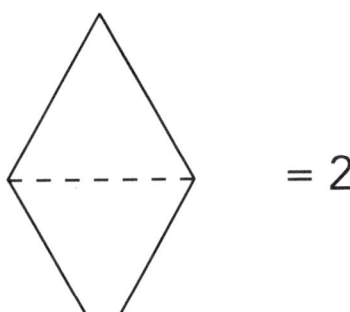 = 2

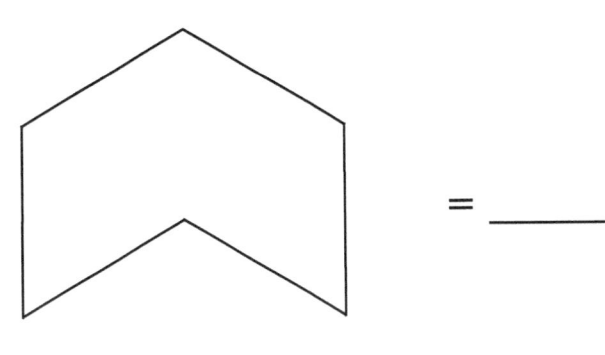 = ____

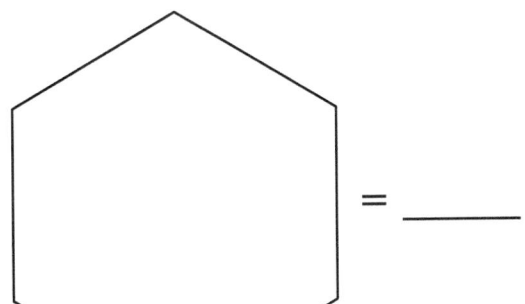 = ____

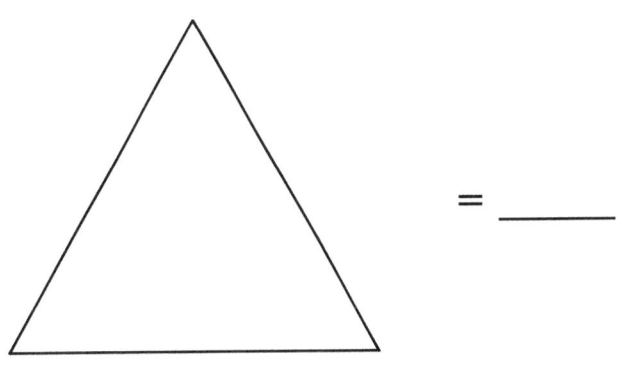 = ____

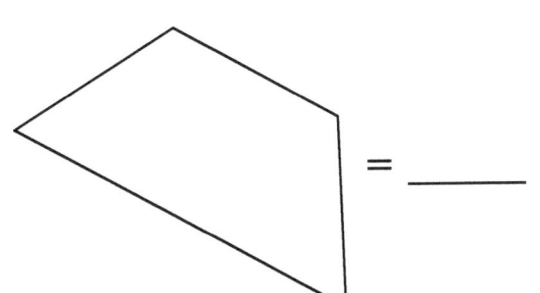 = ____

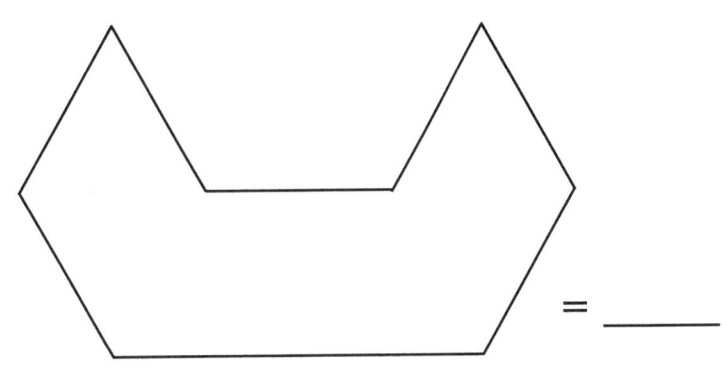 = ____

MEASUREMENT: PERIMETER

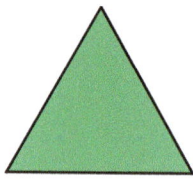 = 3

= 8

 = 4

= 9

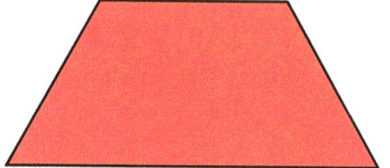 = 5

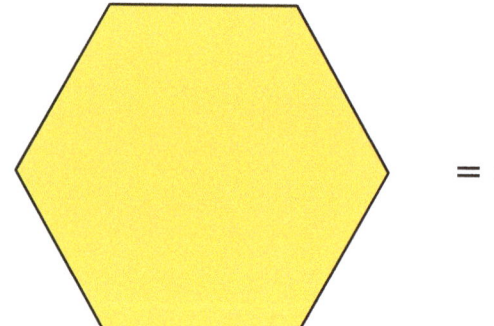 = 6

= 10

= 7

= 12

MEASUREMENT: AREA AND PERIMETER

1)

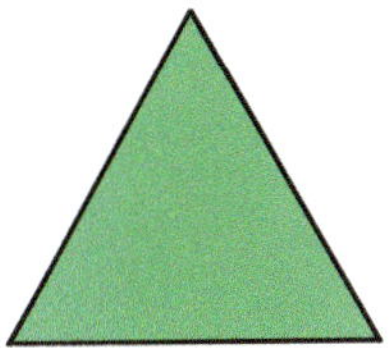

Perimeter _____

Area _____

2)

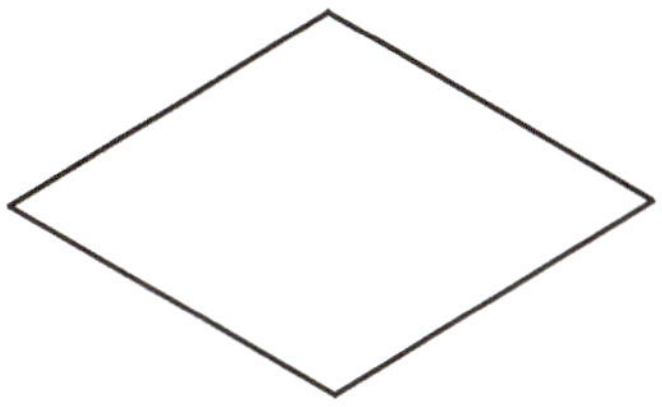

Perimeter _____

Area _____

3)

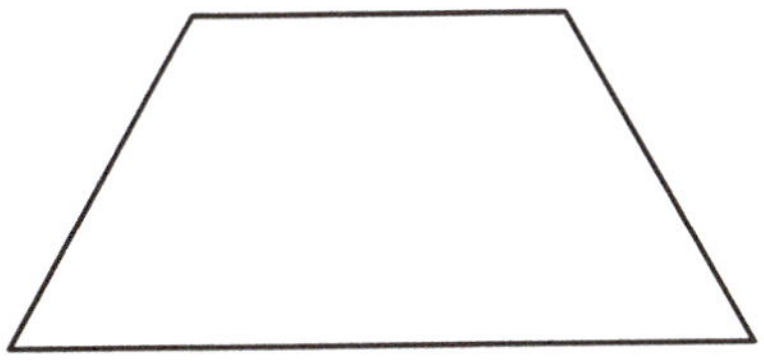

Perimeter _____

Area _____

4)

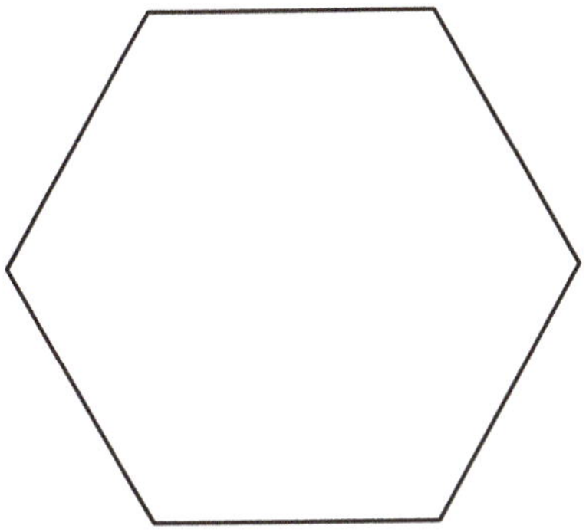

Perimeter _____

Area _____

5)

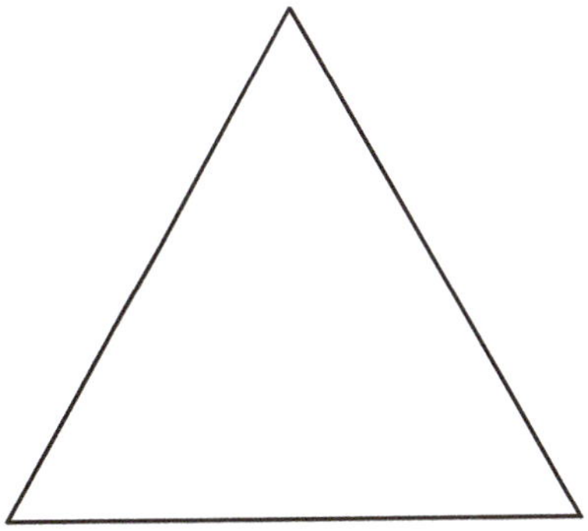

Perimeter _____

Area _____

MEASUREMENT: MORE AREA AND PERIMETER

1)

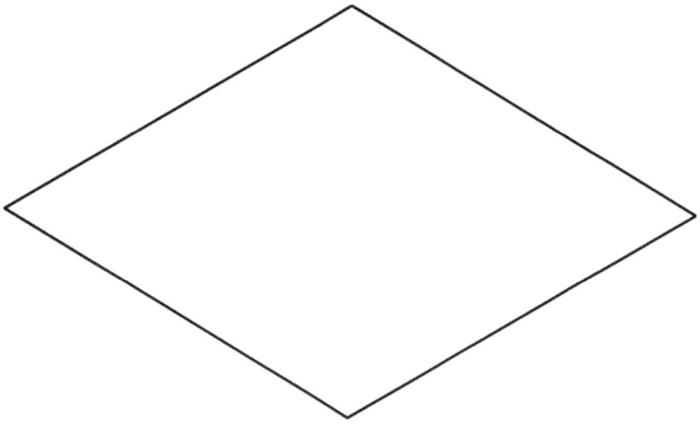

Perimeter _____

Area _____

2)

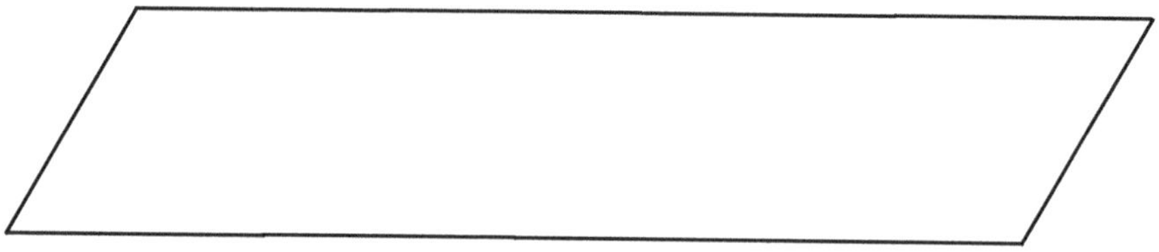

Perimeter _____

Area _____

3)

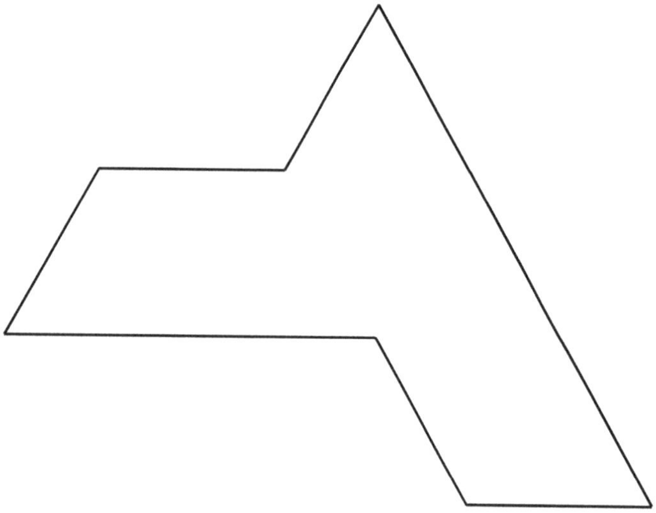

Perimeter _____

Area _____

4)

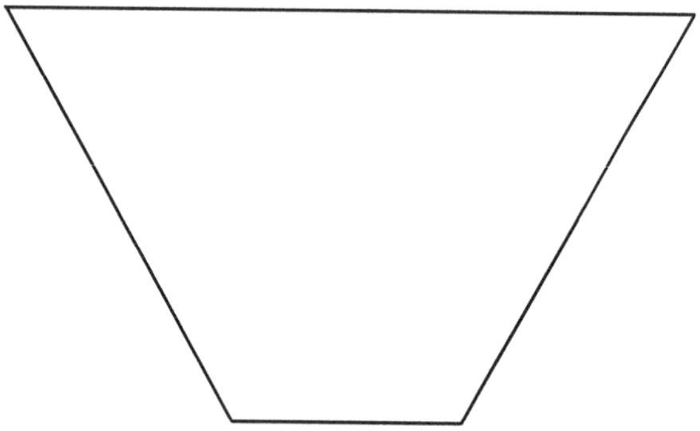

Perimeter _____

Area _____

MEASUREMENT: AREA AND PERIMETER OF VARYING SHAPES

If GREEN = 1 unit of area, draw the following polygons:

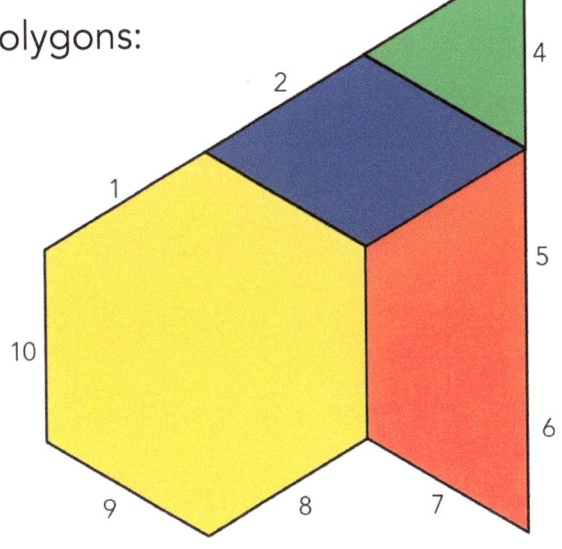

1. Area = 4   Perimeter = 6

2. Area = 6   Perimeter = 6

3. Area = 6   Perimeter = 8

4. Area = 9   Perimeter = 9

5. Area = 8   Perimeter = 8

Completed work should look like this:
Area = 12
Perimeter = 10

NOW YOU TRY!

If BLUE = 1 unit of area, draw the following polygons:

6.   Area = 3   Perimeter = 6

7.   Area = 3   Perimeter = 8

8.   Area = 4   Perimeter = 8

9.   Area = 8   Perimeter = 10

10.   Area = 4   Perimeter = 10

MEASUREMENT: MORE AREA AND PERIMETER OF VARYING SHAPES

If RED = 1 unit of area, draw the following polygons:

11. Area = 2   Perimeter = 8

12. Area = 2   Perimeter = 6

13. Area = 4   Perimeter = 10

14. Area = 5   Perimeter = 17

15. Area = 5   Perimeter = 13

If YELLOW = 1 unit of area, draw the following polygons:

16. Area = 3   Perimeter = 12

17. Area = 4   Perimeter = 14

18. Area = $4\frac{1}{2}$ Perimeter = 17

19. Area = $4\frac{1}{2}$ Perimeter = 15

20. Area = 3   Perimeter = 20

THE TAN RHOMBUS AND SQUARE RATIO

"What is the ratio of the tan rhombus to the square?"

Once children know how to answer this, they can stump adults. For that reason, this is a favorite of children. The children can add, "Is one of the tan rhombuses 1/2 of the square, 1/3 of the square, or some other fraction of the square?"

Prove your answer.

Here is the solution:

- Build these two shapes: The two shapes can be placed on top of each other. They are exactly the same size.
- Try removing the triangle from both of the shapes. They are still equal because the same thing, a triangle, has been removed from both.
- Now it is easy to see that the two tan rhombuses take up the same amount of space as one square.

So, one tan rhombus is 1/2 of the square.

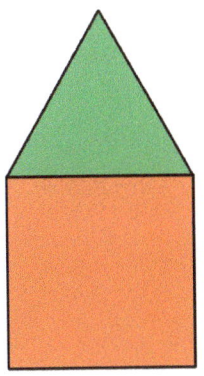

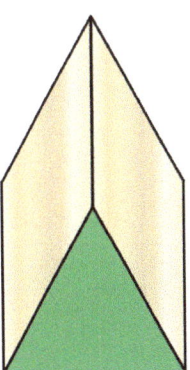

MEASUREMENT: AREA

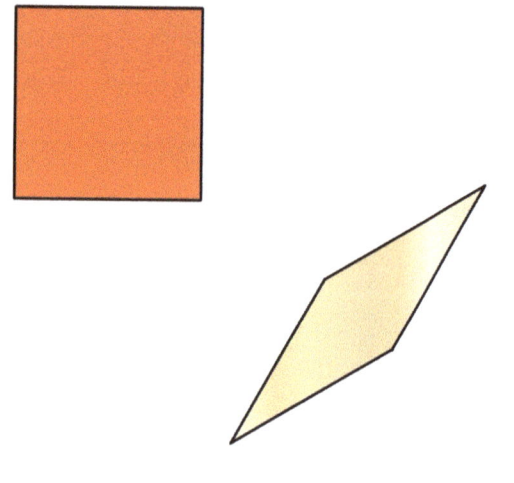

= _____1_____ Area

= _____1/2_____ Area

= _____ Area

= _____ Area

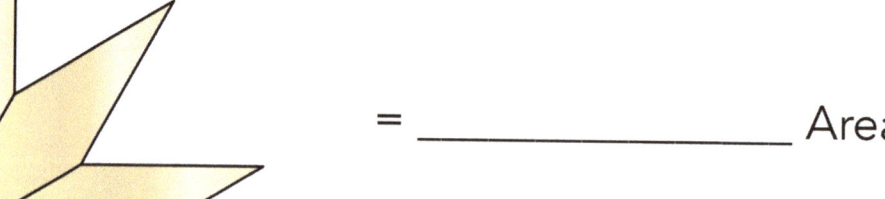

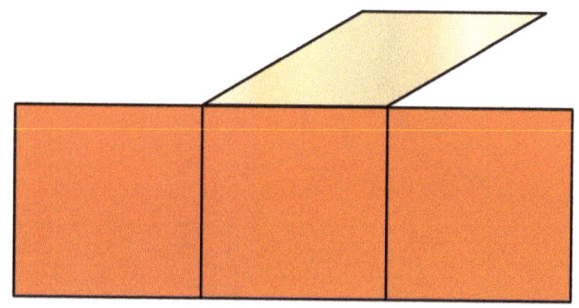

= _____ Area

MEASUREMENT: PERIMETER

 = _____4_____ Perimeter

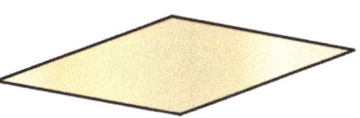 = _____4_____ Perimeter

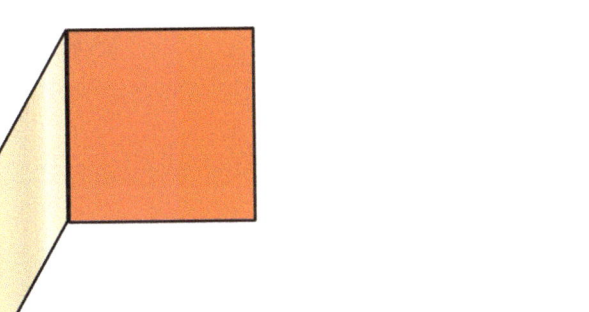 = _____ Perimeter

 = _____ Perimeter

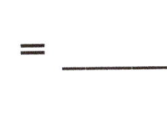 = _____ Perimeter

MEASUREMENT: MORE PERIMETER

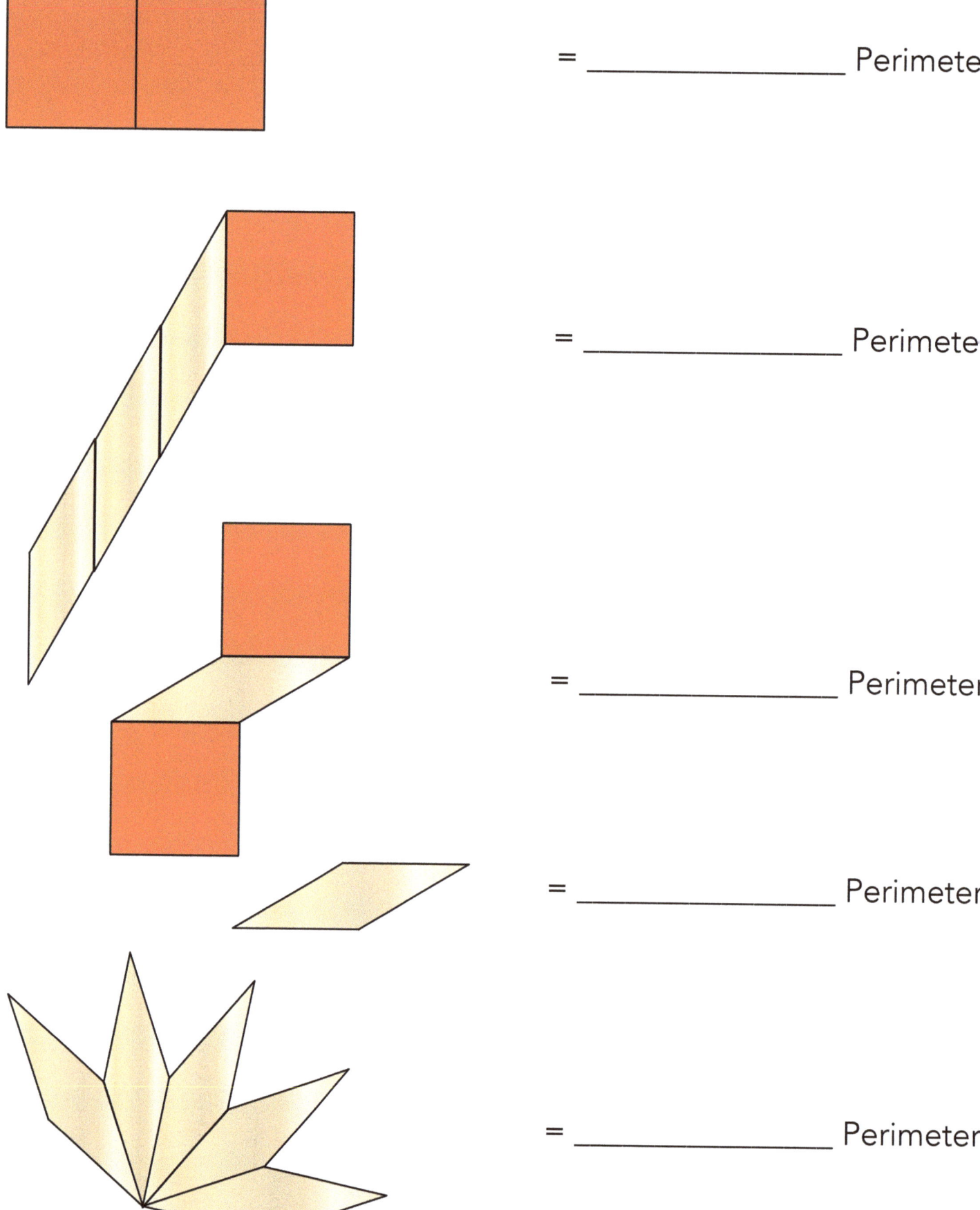

= _____ Perimeter

= _____ Perimeter

= _____ Perimeter

= _____ Perimeter

= _____ Perimeter

FRACTIONS: PART OF A WHOLE

1. Build another animal or item of interest.
2. Reproduce the art with the Pattern Block template and a pencil.
3. Calculate the value of the animal using the scale below
4. Add up all the numerals. This number becomes the denominator of a fraction. *For the example below, our total is 64.*
5. Count the value of triangles and hexagons. *For the example below, 7 triangles are used in the picture, so triangles are 7/64ᵗʰ of the whole picture. Then, 3 hexagons are used in the picture, so the hexagons are 18/64ᵗʰ of the whole picture.*
6. Continue with the remaining 4 shapes. If children are not used to fractions, explain that ½ means 1 out of 2. This 18/64ᵗʰ means 18 out of 64 - the same process as ½.

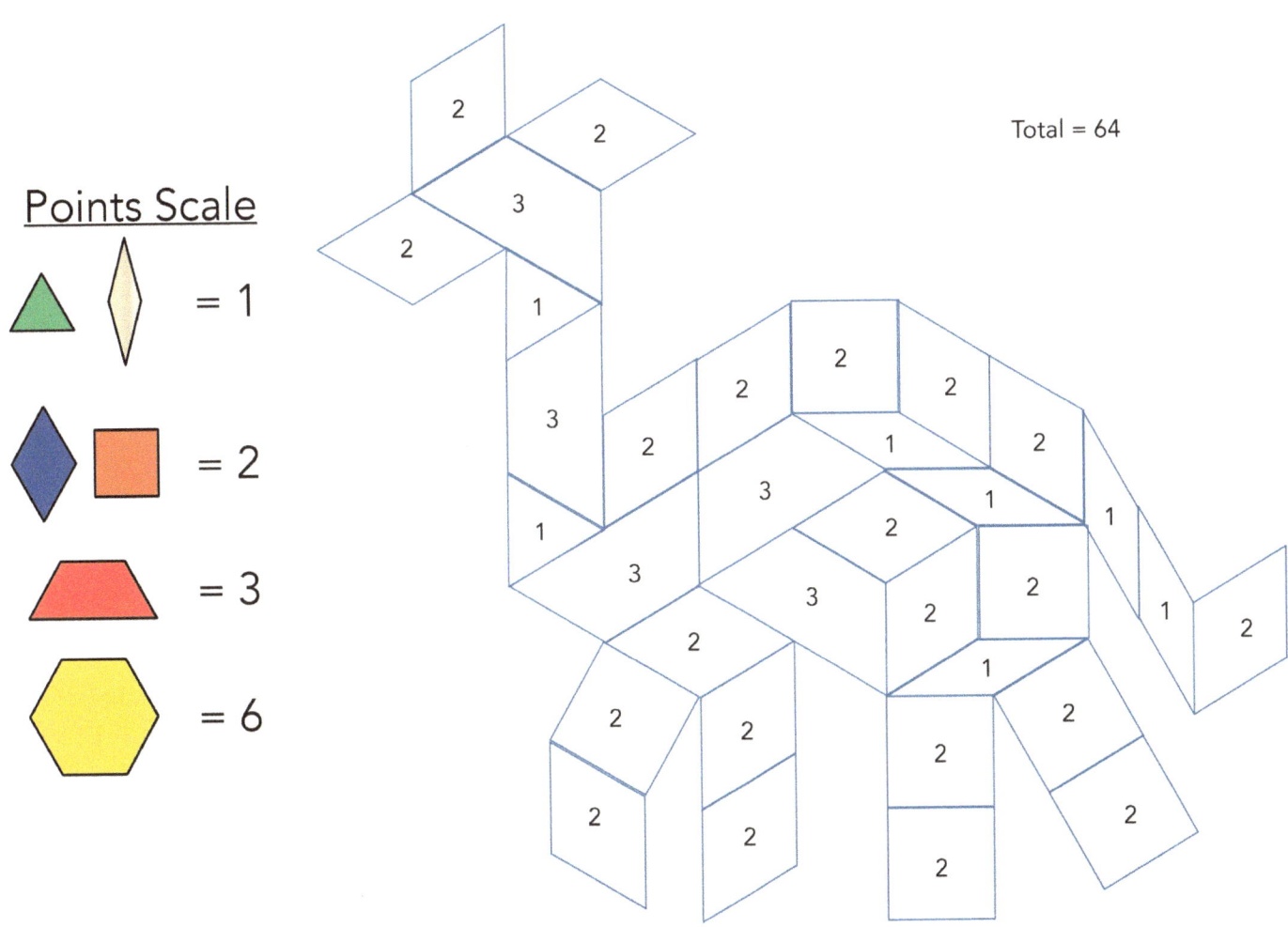

Points Scale

△ ◊ = 1

◆ ■ = 2

▱ = 3

⬡ = 6

Total = 64

FRACTIONS: PART OF A WHOLE, RHOMBUS

Fill the shape with Pattern Blocks of the following colors:

Green, Blue, and Red

(You must use at least one Pattern Block of each color)

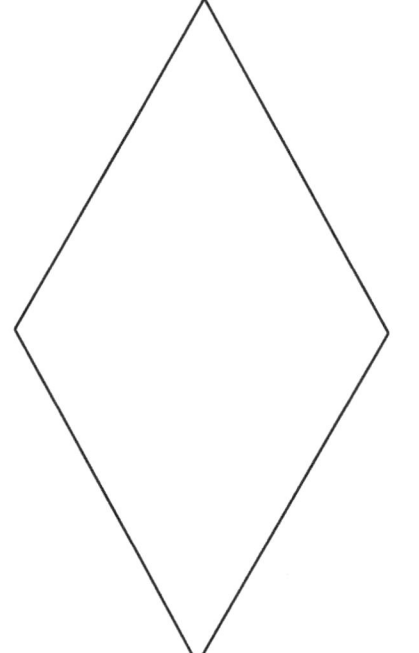

GREEN is _____ of this shape.
(what fraction)

BLUE is _____ of this shape.
(what fraction)

RED is _____ of this shape.
(what fraction)

Order the fractions from least to greatest.

_____ ≤ _____ ≤ _____

Smallest Fraction   Largest Fraction

≤ Means less than or equal

FRACTIONS: PART OF A WHOLE, TRIANGLE

Fill the shape with Pattern Blocks of the following colors:

Green, Blue, and Red

(You must use at least one Pattern Block of each color)

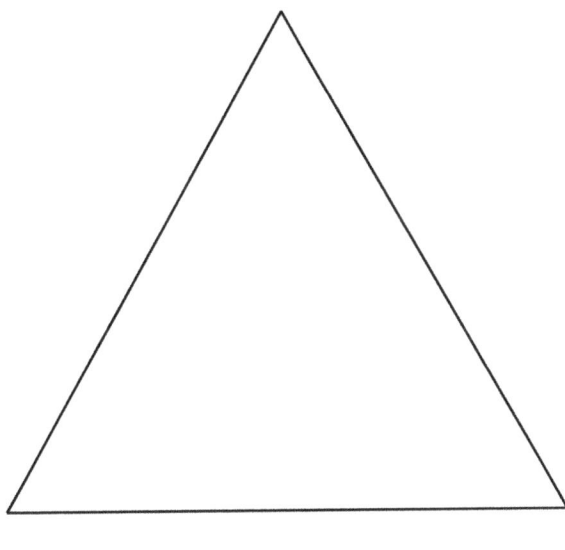

GREEN is _____ of this shape.
(what fraction)

BLUE is _____ of this shape.
(what fraction)

RED is _____ of this shape.
(what fraction)

Order the fractions from least to greatest.

_____ ≤ _____ ≤ _____

Smallest Fraction   Largest Fraction

≤ Means less than or equal

FRACTIONS: PART OF A WHOLE, TRAPEZOID

Fill the shape with Pattern Blocks of the following colors:

Green, Blue, and Red

(You must use at least one Pattern Block of each color)

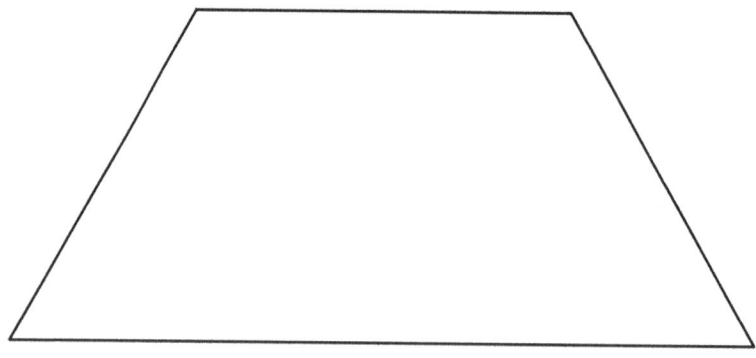

GREEN is _____ of this shape.
(what fraction)

BLUE is _____ of this shape.
(what fraction)

RED is _____ of this shape.
(what fraction)

_____ ≤ _____ ≤ _____

Smallest Fraction   Largest Fraction

≤ Means less than or equal

FRACTIONS: MIXED NUMERALS

Counting is the first way to learn much of mathematics. This is certainly true with fractions. The students will count by ½, ⅓ and ⅙ using Pattern Blocks all the way to 10. When this activity is completed, they will have a much firmer grasp of how fractions work.

For this activity we name the hexagon as 1 and the trapezoid as ½.

The counting begins when the student picks up a trapezoid and writes down ½. Now another trapezoid is picked up and there are two ½'s. The student writes down 2/2 = 1. The process continues with the student picking up trapezoids and writing down the new number.

½
2/2 = 1
3/2 = 1 ½
4/2 = 2
5/2 = 2 ½
6/2 = 3

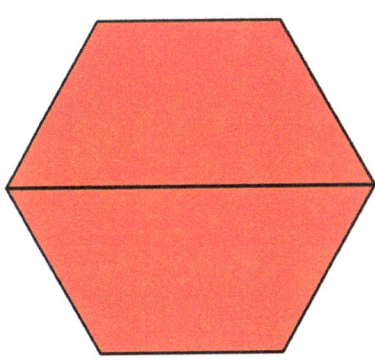

Once the student has completed this fraction activity, the next is counting by ⅓'s with the blue rhombuses.

⅓
⅔
3/3 = 1
4/3 = 1 ⅓
5/3 = 1 ⅔
6/3 = 2

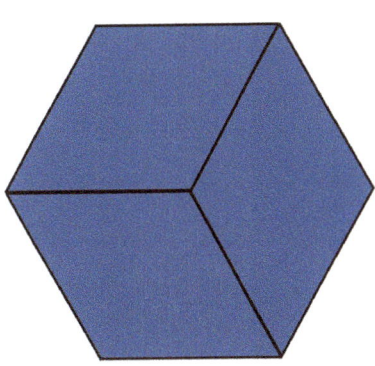

This activity of counting by ½'s, ⅓'s, and ⅙'s all the way to 10 provides a deep understanding of fractions that will suffice for life.

LET'S TRY FRACTIONS WITH MIXED NUMBERS AND IF-THEN LOGIC

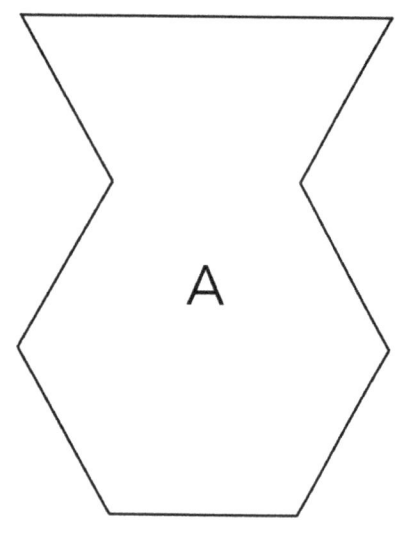

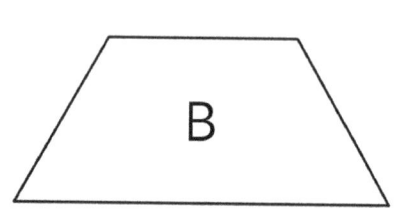

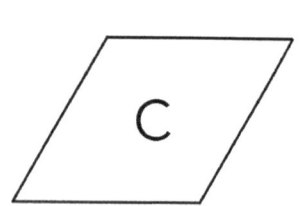

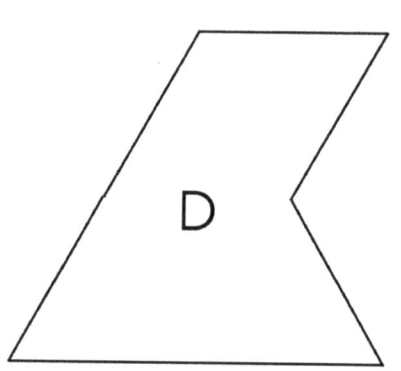

1) If A = 1   THEN   B =   C =   D =

2) If B = 1   THEN   A =   C =   D =

3) If C = 1   THEN   A =   B =   D =

4) If D = 1   THEN   A =   B =   C =

LET'S TRY THESE FRACTIONS WITH MIXED NUMBERS AND IF-THEN LOGIC

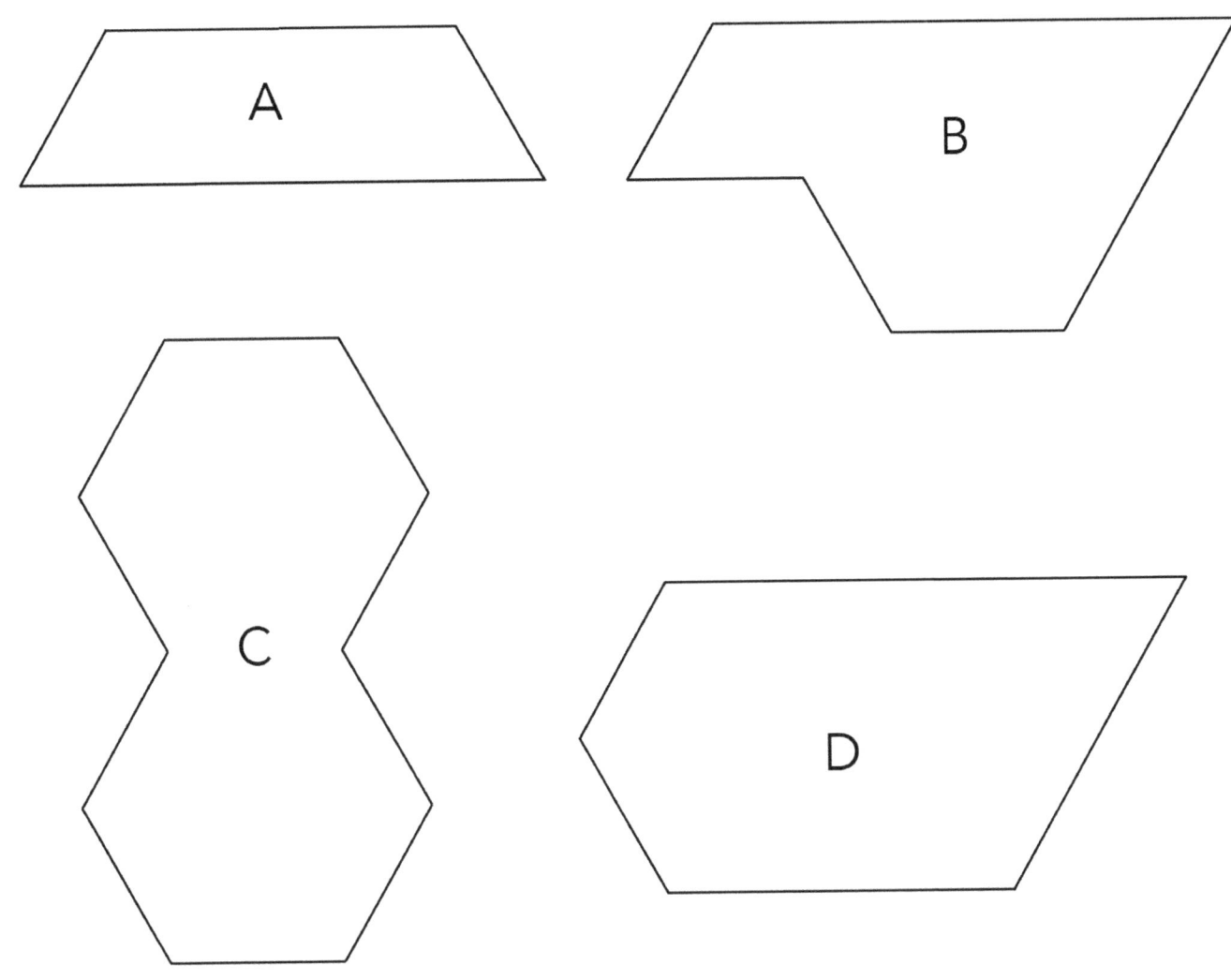

1) If A = 1   THEN   B =   C =   D =

2) If B = 1   THEN   A =   C =   D =

3) If C = 1   THEN   A =   B =   D =

4) If D = 1   THEN   A =   B =   C =

LET'S TRY MORE FRACTIONS WITH MIXED NUMBERS AND IF-THEN LOGIC

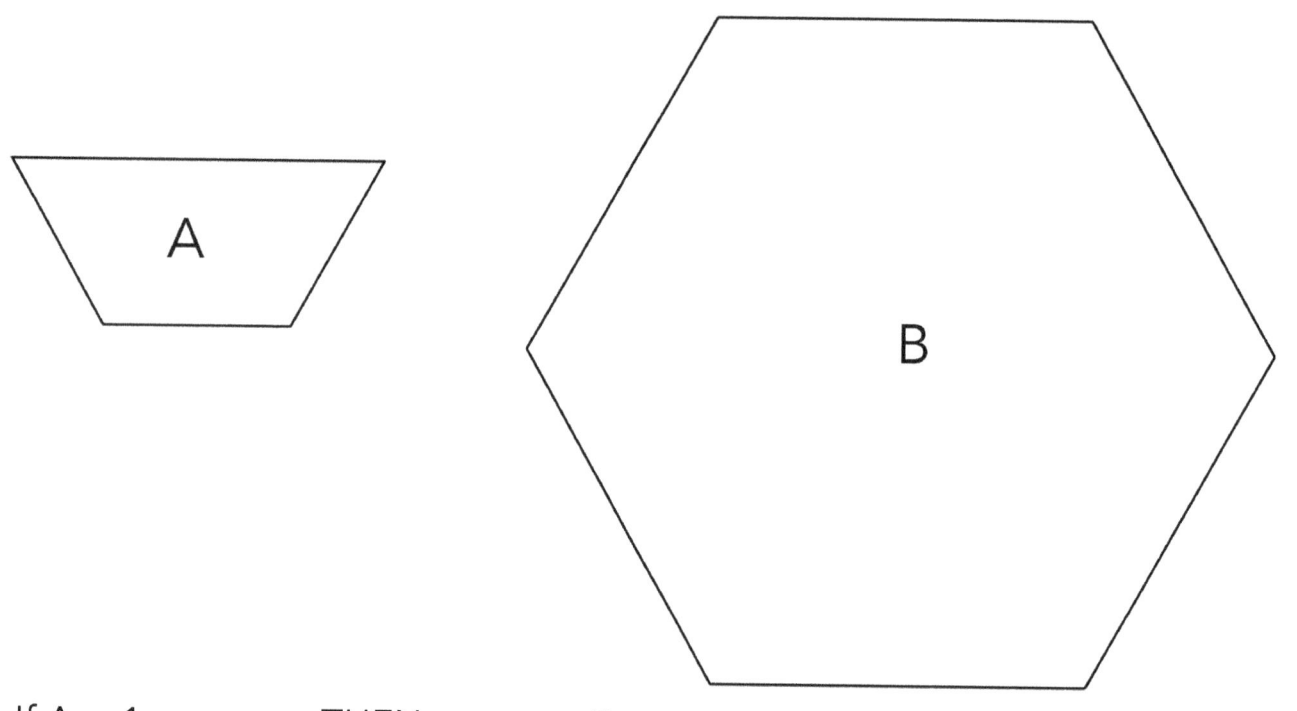

1) If A = 1   THEN   B =   C =   D =

2) If B = 1   THEN   A =   C =   D =

3) If C = 1   THEN   A =   B =   D =

4) If D = 1   THEN   A =   B =   C =

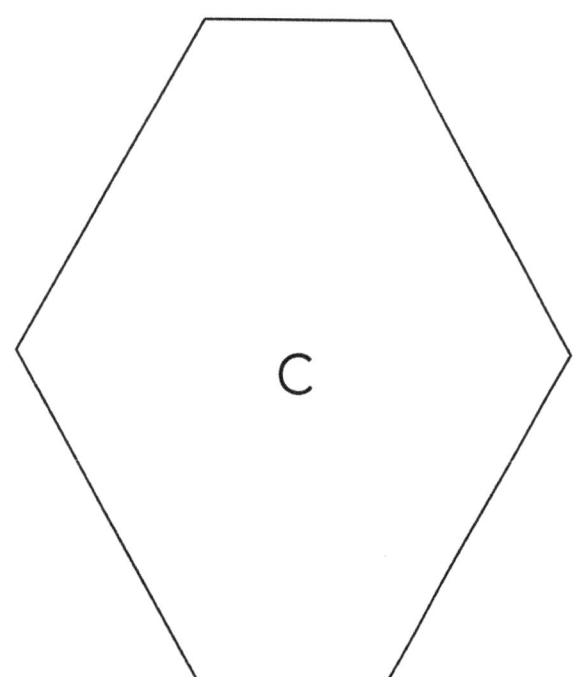

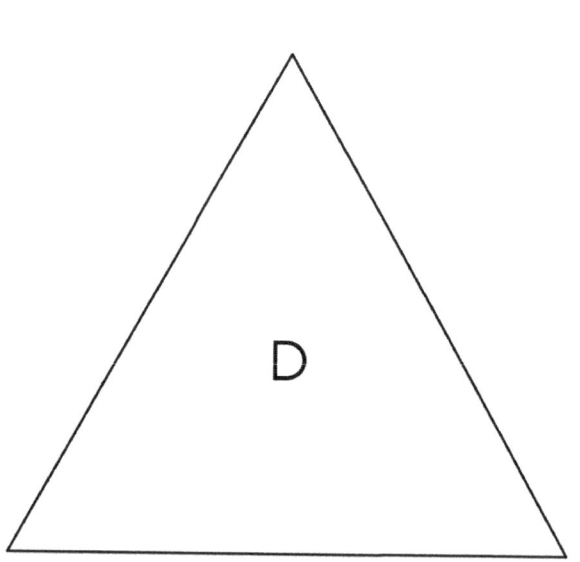

HOW TO CREATE MATH EXPERTS WITH PATTERN BLOCKS

LET'S TRY EVEN MORE FRACTIONS WITH MIXED NUMBERS AND IF-THEN LOGIC

1) If A = 1   THEN   B =   C =   D =

2) If B = 1   THEN   A =   C =   D =

3) If C = 1   THEN   A =   B =   D =

4) If D = 1   THEN   A =   B =   C =

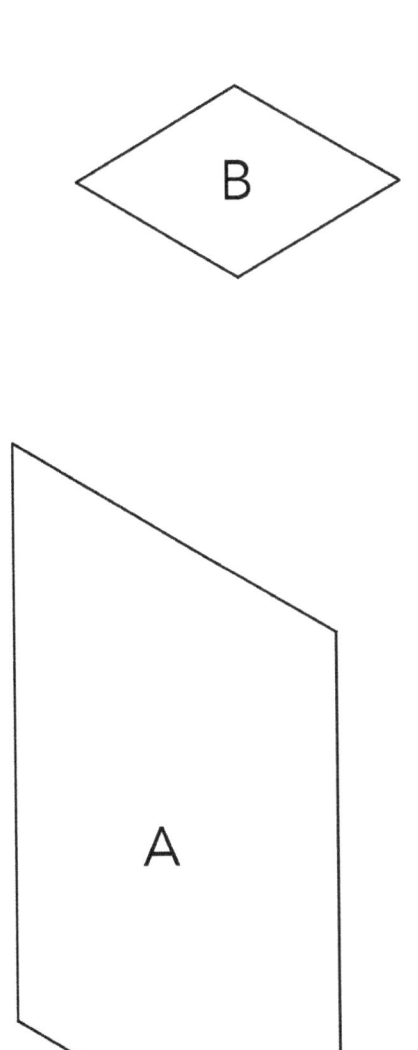

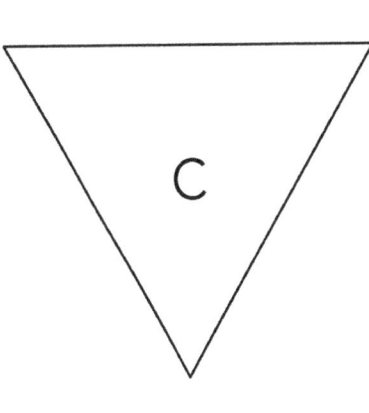

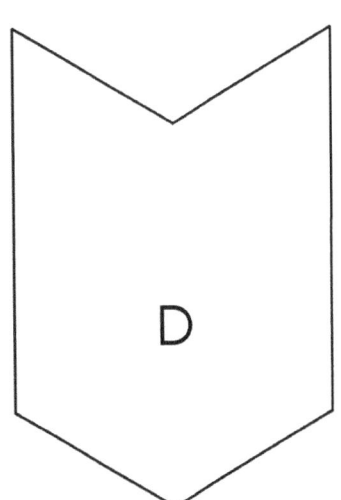

ABOUT THE AUTHORS

Peggy McLean is a Math Specialist for elementary age students. She has traveled across the United States training teachers with the use of manipulative materials to build understanding of mathematical concepts. She knows that teachers must first experience the joy of learning and discovering themselves so that they can share this enthusiasm with children. She says, "Teaching is posing problems more than telling students how to do it."

She holds both Bachelor's and Master's degrees from California State University, San Jose. She taught math, science, and social studies courses for pre-service teachers at Notre Dame de Namur University for 25 years.

Peggy was the Elementary Math Specialist at Nueva School for 45 years and has held the same position at Synapse School for the past 8 years. Peggy's expertise in teaching mathematics is well known by audiences at National Council of Teachers of Mathematics conferences as well as those who were fortunate to learn from her in local school district staff development workshops. Educators who hear that Peggy's books are being updated and published for classroom and home education use express joy that her genius work is still available for a new generation of children. Peggy calls San Carlos, California home.

Dr. Lyle Lee Jenkins is an author, speaker, and recognized authority in improving educational outcomes. He believes that implementing a growth mindset and celebrating progress are the keys to helping students learn more and retain their enthusiasm for school.

His education experience, that spans over 50 years, ranges from working as a teacher, a principal, and a school superintendent to being a University Professor. In 2003, Lyle Lee founded LtoJ, LLC hoping to impact and guide the way we approach education.

Lyle Lee Jenkins has authored six books showcasing continuous improvement in schools, including *How to Create a Perfect School, Optimize Your School, Permission to Forget, From Systems Thinking to Systemic Action, Improving Student Learning*, and *How to Create a Perfect Home School*. All literature offers powerful, practical suggestions for every aspect of education. The two most influential people supporting Dr. Jenkins's work are W. Edwards Deming and John Hattie.

Having spoken to educators all across the United States, Latin America, Europe, Australia, and Asia, Lyle Lee Jenkins is passionate about equipping the next generation with a true love of learning.

Dr. Lyle Lee Jenkins holds a Bachelor of Arts degree from Point Loma Nazarene University, a Masters of Education from San Jose State University and a Ph.D. from The Claremont Graduate University.

Lyle Lee Jenkins's website, www.LtoJ.net, is a great place to discover useful tools to guide your educational journey.

Purchasers of *How to Create Math Experts with Pattern Blocks* may utilize this QR code to download worksheets from this book at no extra cost. This will ease the process of making copies for students. Both the print and digital download versions of this material are protected by copyright laws.